More
Than
Dates &
Dead
People

More

Than

Recovering a
Christian View
of History

Dates &

Dead

STEPHEN L.
MANSFIELD

People

Highland Books

CUMBERLAND HOUSE • NASHVILLE, TN

Published by Cumberland House Publishing, Inc., 431 Harding Industrial
Drive, Nashville, Tennessee 37211.

Cover design by Unlikely Suburban Design, Inc.

Library of Congress Cataloging-in-Publication Data

Mansfield, Stephen, 1958–
    More than dates & dead people : recovering a Christian view of
history / by Stephen L. Mansfield.
        p. cm.
    "Highland Books"
    Includes bibliographical references.
    ISBN 978-1-58182-118-5 (alk. paper) ISBN 978-1-68442-135-0 (hc)
    1. History (Theology) I. Title: More than dates and dead people.
II. Title.
    BR115.H5 M245 2000
    261.5—dc21

This book is dedicated to
my favorite daughter,
Elizabeth,
who is,
as she never ceases to remind me,
my only daughter.

Table of Contents

Foreword

by George Grant

Most people skip all prefaces, forewords, and introductions, so I need not fear that my preliminary comments will somehow spoil what is otherwise a perfectly delightful book. But, if you're one of the rare souls who reads everything—from the sides of cereal boxes to the warranty information that came with your latest CD player—I'm throwing caution to the wind by consuming a few minutes and a few pages to tell you why I think this book deserves our fullest attention. So, please, don't judge the rest of the book by what you read here—it gets better after this. I promise.

First of all, any book that can actually redeem the subject of history from the dust bin of, well, history, is quite a modern marvel and really ought to receive all the attention we can give it. A book that can perform the feat of not just exhuming, but resurrecting all those dry as dust facts from the annals of the past, ought to find its way to the top of our must-read list. It is informative. It is short. It is funny. It is short. It is inspiring. Oh, and did I mention? It is short.

Second, Stephen Mansfield is a really wonderful guy. I know from personal experience. This is not one of those marketing forewords where people who don't really know each other promiscuously toss out all kinds of compliments just for the sake of book sales. *Au contraire.* I actually know him—and I like him anyway. And unlike most of the wonderful guys I know, he is somehow able to convey all his wonderfulness onto the printed page. In other words, he is a really great writer. I think I'd read his books no matter what they were about. Even if I didn't know him.

Third, Dr. Mansfield has his head about him when he is talking about the past. He has an altogether sane perspective of history. You see, he believes that history is a series of lively adventure stories—and thus should be told without the cumbersome intrusion of arcane academic rhetoric or truckloads of extraneous footnotes. In fact, he believes that history is a romantic moral drama in a world gone coldly scientific and impersonal—and thus should be told with passion, unction, and verve. And so he does. His vision of history is down-right fun.

But, fourth, it is also down-right right. He knows that history is inescapably theological—the manifestation of God's good providence in the world. History is indeed "His Story." To Dr. Mansfield, the record of the ages is actually philosophy teaching by example. No matter how social conditions may change, the great underlying qualities which make and save men and nations do not alter, and this is the most important example of all. He thus understands only too well that the past is ever present, giving shape and focus to all our lives. Yet it is not what was, but whatever seems to have been, simply because the past, like the future, is part and parcel of the faith.

And fifth, this compact little manifesto is so well organized that it is sure to find its way into curriculums all across the nation. Its message is perfectly suited for the classroom. It is the sort of tool every teacher loves—a ready-made lesson plan.

For all these reasons—and perhaps a dozen more that I'd best not delineate in any detail lest my foreword dwarf the book itself—I highly commend this volume. In fact, it is my intention to require it of all my students. That way, even if they find my classes altogether unbearable, they'll know it was my fault and not history's. They'll know that history is indeed, *More than Dates and Dead People*. Far more.

Acknowledgements

As I think about those who made this book possible, I wish to thank my first grade teacher for telling my parents that I did not play well with others. The situation was corrected immediately. I wish also to thank Mrs. Cain, my fifth grade teacher, for telling my mother in my presence that I was "immature and retarded." She was half right. Which half is still being determined. Finally, I want to thank Lorraine Ridley, whose flashing blue eyes were the only reason I ever set foot in a high school history class.

More
Than
Dates &
Dead
People

Life in the House of Historical Horrors

I hated history.

I still remember what it was like to walk into my high school history class—that head-swimming, gut-wrenching feeling, the clanging of prison doors behind me, that horrible deer-caught-in-the-headlights look on the faces of my fellow inmates. It was the perfect combination of boredom and terror. Like watching paint dry knowing that the paint could explode at any minute. It was hell. It was abuse. I should sue.

The main reason I hated that history class, though, was none other than Miss Isa Wratchet. Miss Wratchet was my high school history teacher and everything you could possibly want to know about her is summed up in her name—so help me, that was the woman's name! I was sure that Miss Wratchet parked her broom in the faculty parking lot. After all, she was small, hunched over, had a wart on her nose, and usually wore black. So what else was I supposed to think?

Miss Wratchet was a perfect example of that generation of history teachers. These folks assumed that if they just jammed enough dusty details into the vacuous minds of their students something important would happen. Now, they weren't quite sure what that important thing was. Perhaps they thought that if one memorized and crammed and regurgitated, something like "the big picture" would appear miraculously on its own. The idea, it seemed, was that if we learned enough about the trees we would automatically see the forest.

The results are in. It didn't work. Studying history in Miss Wratchet's class was like being lost in a cemetery—dates and dead people, dead people and dates. The more I learned, the less sense it all made. As I sat through this mind-numbing torture, I was sure I heard the very walls groan those ancient words: "Meaningless! Meaningless! Utterly meaningless! Everything is meaningless." Ecclesiastes 1:2, NIV

After a year of this kind of stuff, I concluded that every earthly event of real importance was happening while I was sitting in Miss Wratchet's Chamber of Horrors, not in the distant past. I certainly didn't know much about history, but if the past and what Miss Wratchet was teaching were the same things, I was quite happy to never give either one another thought!

Come to find out, I wasn't alone. Studies show that most Americans hated history class only slightly less than they hated their school lunches. That's bad! But you know what's weird? As much as people hated history class, they still seem to love history. In fact, it seems that people today are more interested in history than ever.

Think about it. Some of the most popular movies of the last few years are about history: *Titanic, Braveheart, Saving Private Ryan, Thin Red Line, Apollo 13, Amistad*—just to name a few.

Television specials, like PBS's The Civil War, tend to break records for the audiences they command. The best-seller list is filled with books on history, historical fiction is at an all-time high in popularity, and we have whole cable networks dedicated to history.

Not only that, Americans hit the highways every year to visit battlefields, museums, dead people's homes, and just about anywhere George Washington did his business. There are even long lines at amusement parks where robots act like presidents, which is fitting when you think about it because it's been the other way around for so long.

Obviously, people are looking for a connection to the past that they never found in the classroom.

In short, history has survived history class. People love the past but hate whatever the heck it was they were forced to study in their local "House of Historical Horrors."

So what was it that made the classroom version of history about as much fun as dental work? How in the world could something so many people love be utterly transformed into something so many people love to hate?

For me the answers to these questions first announced themselves shortly after I left high school. It was then that I became a Christian. It happened probably because every teacher I ever had screamed out at least once, "Oh God, either do something with this kid, or I'll kill him!" So, God did . . . and it was awesome!

Not long after this blessed event, someone told me that there was an owner's manual for this new life. It was called The Bible. Cool. So, I jumped in. And I loved it. I devoured it. I reveled in it. Then late one night I bolted upright in bed with a grand revelation—the *Bible* is . . . gulp . . . history! I was astonished! This book I had come to love so much was filled with history. In fact, I later learned that scholars long ago called it "the divine history." But I didn't hate it. It wasn't like watching paint dry. It wasn't anything like what the Wicked Witch of the West, uh . . . er . . . I mean, Miss Wratchet, tried to teach me. What was the deal?

Then it hit me. History isn't automatically boring. It's the way we look at it that makes it such agony. If we look at it the right way then we can see it for what it is and history can become much more than dates and dead people.

As this massive truth entered my peewee-sized brain, it happened. A light shone all around me. I fell to my knees. Angels sang. The deer pranced, and the birds chirped, and all about me was . . . well, like a Disney cartoon. Anyway, at that moment I heard a voice say, "Go forth, learn, and show others the way."

So . . . here goes!

History & the Monkeys

The Critters, Not the Rock Group

Some people say that our problem with history starts with the way we use the word.

When someone dies, we say, "He's history."

In sports, when someone fouls out, strikes out, falls out, gets knocked out, or just plain drowns, some obnoxious announcer shouts, "He's outta heaa! He's history!"

When someone brings up a terribly embarrassing moment from our past, they usually try to comfort us by saying, "It's over. It's all ancient history now."

So who wants to dive into this kind of stuff?

Then there are some serious thoughts on the matter.

Some people believe our problem is more about meaning. Of all the subjects we study in school, history never seems to suggest right up front a good reason for learning it. We know that we study English, math, government, science, and even physical education because they somehow relate to our daily lives. They give us tools for living.

But learning about the past seems to have almost no practical purpose at all. What difference does it make what Thomas

Jefferson did or why Martin Luther ate a diet of worms or why a bunch of travel agents had it out at the Battle of Tours? Seriously, what does any of this have to do with me? And, if no one ever explained why we should learn history—why it was important in the first place—then we were not likely to learn it, or at least learn it well. So we didn't! This is obvious since studies show that Americans learn more history by accident from TV mini-series than they ever did in history class.

Some think our problem is even simpler than this. Usually, human beings are fascinated by other human beings. We love to read about, talk about, watch movies about, and hear juicy tidbits about other folks. Even in childhood we love stories about other people—about wicked villains and heroes who get the girl. So, unless someone messes it up for us, history should be fun. History is, after all, simply the story of people and what they do . . . or did.

But in most history classes, it's "The Age of This" and "The Era of That"—social transformation, class struggle, industrial revolution, dialectics, economic interpretations. It's cold and impersonal, like airplane food: no spice, no inspiration.

It's like those *Bibles* that you know were printed by people who never expected anyone to read them. The print is microscopic, the paper is so thin you can read the next six pages without turning the first page, and the really important stuff is printed in a color incapable of detection by the human eye. They couldn't have made *Bible* reading more difficult if they tried!

The same is true of history class. All they had to do was build on every child's natural interest in things like cowboys and Indians, distant lands, pirates, beautiful women, castles, kings and queens, wars, spies, families in wagon trains, and . . . did I mention beautiful women? But it's just like those *Bibles*. History class seemed like it was carefully designed to snuff out any natural interest in the past that may be lurking in our minds. And it worked . . . perfectly.

Now, all of these suggestions might be true. After all, folks much smarter than us get paid big bucks to sit around, smoke their pipes, and think great thoughts about such matters. Still, I think they've missed something. I think there must be something that explains why history class was boredom on stun, why every minute in that classroom was like fingernails on a chalkboard.

I think they were teaching us history according to the monkeys—the critters, not the rock band.

You see, when you study history in a typical school today, the books you read, the lectures you hear, and the conclusions you're supposed to make are all conditioned by a certain philosophy. The people who write those books and plan your studies design what you are supposed to learn according to a certain set of principles, a certain view of the world. And that view is rooted in the philosophy of evolution. And evolution is the monkey version of history.

Let's think about it. What does evolution teach? Evolution is the idea that life happened accidentally. Supposedly, the accidental mixing of some biological goo billions of years ago gave birth to the first living cell. In time, that cell grew into a critter. I won't bore you with technical language. Then, there were suddenly lots and lots of critters. In time, those critters grew into man-like critters—namely, monkeys and apes—and eventually into cappuccino drinking, cell phone-toting, city-dwellers.

Ah, but let's think about what this means to our experience in the House of Historical Horrors. In other words, what does believing in evolution mean for the study of history?

First, according to evolutionary theory, all of life is an accident. There is no design or purpose. Everything just is—with no meaning, no pattern, no destination. Everything is random.

Secondly, notice that according to evolution, everything is growing from very simple to increasingly complex—from the outdated to the new and improved. This means that what is old is not as good as what is new. Old is simple and goofy, while new is shiny and sophisticated. This means that the past is less important than today, and today will be less important than tomorrow.

Well, no wonder history class is so boring! If evolution provides the philosophy we use to understand the past (and it does, because evolution is the official public school explanation for what exists), then it only makes sense that history is going to seem like a silly thing to learn. After all, why should we study a time long ago that has less to say to us than our own time? That's like asking your baby brother about the really important issues of life—like where babies come from and how you know the light goes off in the refrigerator when you close the door. You wouldn't think of asking him these things because he's not as smart as you are, not as good looking or as wise. In other words, he's not as evolved. That's just how evo-lution tells us to look at the past.

Why study anything that's made by accident? That's like throwing a box full of dice onto a basketball court and then spending years trying to find some meaning in the way the dice landed. There isn't any! It's all random, and that's the way it is when we view the past through the lens of evolution. All is accident. All is chance. All is less important than today, except tomorrow. Nothing is absolute. Nothing is certain. According to evolution, what happened in the past doesn't have any real bearing on or meaning for us today.

But if this kind of history can't teach us anything, what is it? Simple. It's dates and dead people on stun!

So, the Miss Isa Wratchets of the world are teaching some-thing that their own philosophy says has no meaning. They only teach it because the government says there has to be a history class. Or they teach it because it helps to burn an evolutionary view of the world into the minds of unsuspecting students. Or maybe they teach it because they're really interested in it even though they don't think it has any great meaning. Whatever the reason, this is why we'd rather be blowing up things in science class any day of the week than spending one hour in the spooky cemetery of a typical history class.

But there is good news. Remember that owner's manual, the *Bible,* that I discovered after I became a Christian? I dis-covered in it something that rescued history from the abyss of evolution and made learning about the past fascinating, inspiring, and life-changing.

What was it? It's really quite simple. History isn't an accident. It isn't meaningless. Why? Because God made history and gave it meaning!

Sound too good to be true? Then keep reading . . .

History According to the Owner's Manual

So there I was just out of high school, and suddenly I find out that there really is a God. And He even had a book out. Unbelievable! Then, when I start reading His best seller, I find out some really astounding stuff.

See, when you read the *Bible,* it isn't hard to figure out that God created the world and put man in it. That's a "no brainer." After all, the Bible tells us that in the first few pages. But the Bible goes on to tell us that God not only created the world, He runs it. He's in charge. He determines what happens. To use the big boy word, He's sovereign. In other words, the world is His and what happens takes place because He wants it to.

Pretty big statement, huh? I thought so. But that's what the *Bible* says. Check it out. Take a minute to look up these scriptures in your *Bible.* -

1. God does what he wants with the people
    of the earth—Daniel 4:35
2. God establishes all government and all
    authority—Romans 13:1

3. God directs what kings and rulers
    do—Proverbs 21:1
4. God puts rulers in place and he disposes of
    them when he wants to—Daniel 2:21
5. God determines where men live and the borders
    of nations—Acts 17:26
6. God determines the times set for men—Acts 17:26
7. God controls the weather—Psalm 148:8 and
    Psalm 147:8, 15–18
8. God controls the times and the
    seasons—Daniel 2:21
9. God controls the animals—Psalm 8:6–8
10. God creates disaster and prosperity—Isaiah 45:7
11. God determines the outcomes of
    wars—Proverbs 21:31

Get the picture? All the stuff that history is about—the rise and fall of nations, wars, what great leaders do, disasters, great migrations of people, explorations, inventions—all of these are under God's control. Pretty amazing, isn't it? So, if all these things are true (remember, this is God's Word we're talking about, so it must be true), then what we call history is actually a stage, and on that stage God directs the action according to His own script. This changes everything! This means that history isn't just random and meaningless. This means that evolution is wrong. God makes history. God rules history. God gives history its meaning.

To put it another way, history is really like a gigantic tapestry. God is weaving that tapestry to make a picture He has in mind. We can't see the whole pattern clearly from our vantage point. We see history like we're looking at the back of that tapestry. You can sort of see an image, but there's all that loose string and glue and weird-looking and criss-crossed stitching. Only when the work is finished will we really understand what God has been doing. Until then, we have to take God's word for it. He's making history what He wants it to be.

Wow! That really changes everything.

But there's more . . .

Back to the Future

Once we get the idea that God rules history, some other truths about history start to land. But watch out! Some of these truths are real mind benders. This is just because we're used to the monkey version of history—history according to evolution. The truth seems weird when you've believed a lie for so long.

Now, you have to really think about this one.

If history really is a stage and if God really is directing the action on that stage, then it's the final act—when everything is resolved and all secrets are revealed— that gives the play it's meaning. Or, to say it another way, it's what God wants history to be when it ends that determines everything else that happens in history. Or, to say it even another way, it's the future that powers the past.

Okay, I warned you. But stick with me.

It may be easier to understand this idea if we use what the *Bible* says about you as an illustration.

Before you were even born into this world, God had already determined His ultimate purpose for your life. Another word for this purpose is "calling." God decided before you were even conceived what the finished product of your life, what this calling, would be. For example, God told Jeremiah that He had appointed him as a prophet to the nations before Jeremiah was even conceived (Jeremiah 1:5, NIV).

Once your calling was decided and God's perfect time for you to be born came along, God formed you in the womb and gave you both your body and your own distinct personality. He even determined the number of days you would live before you had even lived a single one of them. He did all this in light of what He had already called you to be (Psalm 139:16, NIV).

Then, after you were born, God began to try to "take hold" of you, to draw you to Himself, so that you could start to "take hold" of His purposes for your life (Philippians 3:12, NIV). Ever since you were born, God has been shaping your life so that you can fulfill your destiny—the purpose He set for your life before you were born. So your destiny, your ultimate calling, is what decides the course of your life.

This is exactly how it is with history, too. God didn't just wind up the clock of history so that it could run without any meaning until it finally runs down. Instead, He first decided what is going to happen at the end—what the destiny for all of history is. To say it another way, He decided the future first. Then, beginning with creation, God began to draw mankind through the ages to a final destiny. It is God's future that gives history its driving force and its meaning.

This sounds strange to us because we're used to a monkey version of history. We live in a world filled with evolutionary thinking. Evolution teaches that the future is a blank and that man is pushed forward by the past. The past determines the present, and the future is a dark and mysterious blank. As one scholar has written, "Evolutionary time emerges out of the past, gropes its way blindly into the present, and moves sightlessly into an unknown future."

To those who understand that history is God's creation, though, history isn't the story of blind men groping toward a dark and fearful future. Instead, it's the unfolding of a future— a beautiful tapestry—that God decided upon before the creation of the world. This gives us hope. It also makes history a wild ride, but one that never gets out of God's control.

But hang on. There's still more . . .

Living in a Cardboard Tube

So, God rules history, and He rules it according to how He wants it to end. Not too painful, huh? But get ready for this next one.

The Bible tells us that history exists in the middle of a thing called eternity. Now, you probably don't do much thinking about eternity until you have to sit through something *reeaaally boorrring*. Then you're pretty sure you know what eternity is all about!

But the concept of eternity is extremely important for us to understand because it's what gives history its meaning. Without understanding eternity, we can't understand history.

So, here we go.

God lives in a realm called eternity. This realm has no beginning or end. In this thing called eternity, time does not exist like it does in history (Psalm 93:2, NIV; Isaiah 57:15, KJV). In eternity, everything is "now." There's no past or future. Everything is experienced the way we experience the present. Also, eternal things don't age or die. Time simply has no power in eternity.

This is because God created time as a unique characteristic of history—the realm in which we live. In our existence, time plays a powerful role. We experience a past, a present, and a future. Things in history are born, grow old, and then die. We live time progressively and chronologically, passing through weeks and months and years. Time is a major part of our existence.

But what we call "time" or "history," God sees all at once from the beginning to the end. God, being an eternal God and dwelling in eternity, is not limited to experiencing time like we do. He experiences everything as the present, knowing the end from the beginning (Isaiah 46:10, NIV).

Okay, shake the cobwebs out, and let's look at this another way.

Think of eternity as a vast, unending space. It moves out in every conceivable direction and never stops. Now, in the middle of this vast expanse of eternity, picture a glass tube or maybe a cardboard tube like the kind that comes in the center of a roll of paper towels. Let's say this tube is history. Scholars would call this tube a "space/time continuum," but we'll keep it simple and just call it a "tube." Scholars, after all, get paid for taking simple things and making them ridiculously complex.

God created history and, like the tube, it has a beginning and an end. The beginning is creation and the end is the end of all time. Inside of this tube, human beings live and experience time one minute, one day, and one century at a time. You look "back" on the past, you live today in the "present" and you look "forward" to tomorrow. It's as though you're living along a line— like the line down the center of a road. You start, you drive along the road one mile at a time, and you come to the end. This is how we experience time in the "tube" of history. This is how we live our lives.

But as soon as you step out of history, out of this tube, you're in eternity. Time and its effects are no more. Everything is "now," and you can look at the tube, at history, from beginning to end in one glance. This is what happens when you die.

Okay, so why is any of this important?

First, history and eternity aren't the same thing. Most people think that history will go on forever, but it won't. Remember, the tube comes to an end. God created history for specific purposes, and when these purposes are fulfilled, history is over.

Secondly, God played a trick on us. He put our bodies in the tube of history, but the *Bible* says He put eternity in our hearts (Ecclesiastes 3:11). This means that we can never be fully comfortable in the tube of history because at our core we are eternal creatures. He made us for eternity. History is just where we live until we get there. We're just passing through.

This is important, because it explains why all throughout history we find men trying to reach outside the tube, trying to touch the eternal. This may also help to explain all the different religions in the world. The problem is that we all feel like misfits in history because when God put eternity in our hearts, he ruined us for this life alone. We hunger for more than this life has to offer. Still, history is full of men trying to make what happens in the tube match what eternity is like. Of course, it can't happen, but that doesn't keep men from trying.

Finally, we have to keep in mind how short history is in the scheme of things—not to mention how short each human lifetime is. The *Bible* uses words like "vapor" and "momentary" to describe human lifetimes. Since life is so short, it must be because eternity is the real meaning of everything. In other words, we need to measure everything in history in terms of eternity. We have to keep eternity in mind when we think about everything inside the tube—in history. Thinking this way helps us live our lives and think about history with an eternal perspective. This way, we don't miss "The Point."

The Empire Strikes Back

Okay, let's see how far we've come. So far we've talked about three important truths—let's call them pillars—for understanding history in a biblical light.

First, God rules what happens in history.

Secondly, God has a destination for history that gives everything else in history it's meaning.

Thirdly, history is a time tube in the middle of eternity.

So far, so good.

But there's one more pillar we have to put in place. This fourth truth explains much of what happens in history and, in a sense, explains what history is all about. And here it is: to understand history from a biblical perspective, we have to realize that history is in large part shaped by the conflict between two spiritual kingdoms that are vying for control of mankind.

Sound strange? Don't worry. It'll make sense. Now, let's see how this works.

Most people who believe in God basically assume that there's God and there's mankind and that's it. But that's not what God says. The *Bible* tells us that there's another player in the game. His name is Satan, and he isn't a happy camper.

So who is this dude? The *Bible* tells us that Satan started out as a high-ranking angel in heaven. He probably even ministered before the throne of God and may have had something to do with the worship that goes on in heaven. Eventually, though, Satan got the big head, thought he was greater than God, and got booted out of heaven. Jesus said He saw Satan fall from heaven like lightening (Isaiah 14:12–15, NIV; Luke 10:18, NIV).

So what's Satan doing now? The *Bible* teaches that Satan, or Lucifer, is now the head of a kingdom of his own (Matthew

12:26, NIV). This kingdom is devoted to ruling the earth with evil. Satan and his demons, the name for angels that fell from heaven with their leader, work to control mankind through deception and the manipulation of human passions. This kingdom is devoted to the effort of killing, stealing, and destroying both God's kingdom and all of mankind. Its tactics are hatred, fear, and deception.

Satan is especially worried about keeping everyone he dominates away from God's kingdom, so he blinds them spiritually and offers lots of snazzy counterfeits (2 Corinthians 4:4, NIV). These are what the *Bible* speaks of as false miracles, false angels, false christs, false gospels, and false gods.

This kingdom of darkness, however, is actually just Satan's rather shabby copy of God's kingdom. Satan is an imitator who designed his weak, rebellious kingdom after what he saw in the kingdom of God back before he got zapped.

Now, what is strange about this conflict between the kingdom of God and the kingdom of darkness is that it's already decided. The *Bible* teaches that Satan was defeated when Jesus rose from the dead. Right then Satan was disarmed—stripped of all his power (Colossians 2:15, NIV). Today, the kingdom of darkness is an outlaw kingdom—like a band of guerillas that won't give up. Satan and his forces go around trying to take over human lives and even nations, but ultimately they aren't going to win.

Even though this conflict is already decided, it still has a huge impact on the course of history. Think about it. If it is true that history is the battleground between two kingdoms, one evil and one good, then this would explain a lot about what has happened in the past.

For example, could it be that Adolf Hitler and the Nazis weren't just a bunch of guys who hated Jews and wanted to rule the world? Suppose that what Hitler did, and really, all of what happened in World War II, was actually a result of this battle we're talking about between two kingdoms. Suppose that Satan thought up the Nazi philosophy, and his goal was to kill millions of people, produce generations of hatred and fear, wipe out the Jews, permanently compromise the Christian Church, and change the whole course of human history. This may sound strange, but when you realize that behind the scenes the Nazis were deeply into the occult and Satan worship (it's true!), you can also see that what happened on earth during World War II may well have been the result of the spiritual battle between God and Satan.

When you start thinking about history as a spiritual battleground, you can look at the past from an entirely different perspective. You start seeing that human wars mirror spiritual wars. You start looking at every idea, philosophy, or religion in light of the kingdom it comes from. You start to see the battle that is raging for the soul of every person and the soul of every nation. And you start to understand why history is filled with such beauty and grace at the same time it is filled with such barbarity and horror.

Now What?

So, these are the four pillars of a Christian view of history. God rules history. God orchestrates history according to how He wants it to end. History gets its meaning from eternity. History is a battleground between two spiritual kingdoms—God's kingdom and the evil empire of Satan.

What a difference these four simple truths make! History isn't the meaningless confusion that evolution leads us to believe. Instead, it's the stage for the most thrilling drama ever—a drama completely under God's control.

Now, if we really believe this, it shouldn't just change the way we think about history. It should also change the way we live. If what the *Bible* says about history is true, then knowing history should have a massive impact on who we are. So, let's look at some ways that history, viewed from a Christian perspective, should change our lives.

Armed and Dangerous

Using History to Make a Life Worth Living

Most of the subjects we study in school seem to come with a good reason for learning them. We study math to help us keep a checkbook balanced or to figure out our batting average. We study English because it helps our dating life. Right? We even study science because it has a vague relationship to stuff we do under a car or in a kitchen. We expect a practical benefit, and we can get it from each of these subjects.

But when it comes to history, we're not so sure. Especially if we think about history from an evolutionary perspective, there doesn't seem to be a good reason for all the suffering we have endured to learn about the past. And, as we've already said, from an evolutionary perspective, there really aren't very many good reasons to study history. From a biblical perspective, though, the whole picture changes. Suddenly knowing the past becomes amazingly practical. In fact, it can change your life. Let's see how.

Seeing God

A work of art will tell you a great deal about the artist who created it. A painting by Norman Rockwell or a song by Paul McCartney or a dance by Alvin Ailey or a poem by Longfellow tells you a great deal about each of these people. Art reveals the artist. In the same way, creation reveals the Creator. What God makes reveals who He is. In fact, the *Bible* teaches us that the world God made reveals him so clearly that men don't have any excuse for not believing in Him. Listen to Romans 1:19–20, "Since what may be known about God is plain to them (the wicked), because God has made it plain to them. For since the creation of the world God's invisible qualities—His eternal power and divine nature—have been clearly seen, being understood from what has been made, so that men are without excuse."

Now, the big boy phrase for this is called, "natural revelation." It means that God shows us who He is through nature or what He has made. It means that mountains and trees and animals and stars and oceans tell us things about the God who made them. In fact, this means there shouldn't be any atheists, because God makes Himself plain to all men.

This truth reminds me of an experience I had with my grandmother, who was both a famous artist and a native American. She had an unusual insight into nature. She could "read" nature the way some people read other human beings. I remember one day I walked into her kitchen and found her holding a tomato with tears in her eyes. I asked her what was wrong. She told me that when she sliced open the tomato and saw the intricate design and detail inside, she was overcome with the wonder of God. At the time I thought she had flipped out. But later, after I became a Christian, I understood that she had simply tapped into what God has to say through what He has made.

So what does this have to do with history? Simple. If what God makes reveals who He is, and history is one of the things God has made, then history should help us see God. And it does. Just like God can be seen in oceans and mountains and tomatoes, He can also be seen in how nations rise or how wars are fought or how great leaders change the world. History really is "His story," and this means that knowing history in a biblical light is a way of getting to know God and how He works.

The Power of a Heritage

If I could convince you that your ancestors had all been thieves, murderers, or rapists—in short, the most evil and disgusting sort of people—it would change the way you see yourself, wouldn't it? And seeing yourself differently would change the way you live, right?

Likewise, if I could convince you that you are descended from royalty—from a long line of great rulers and conquerors—this would change you, too.

The fact is that the way you see your past has a lot to do with the way you see yourself now. And the way you see yourself, good or bad, determines the way you live. This is why we say that history has the power to impart a sense of destiny. Your view of your past will shape your view of your future, and this is not only true of individuals, but even of nations—in fact, of any group of people.

This is one of the reasons history is so important. God has made us with a need to see ourselves as part of something ongoing, something which was around before we were and which will be here long after we are gone.

Because God created man with this great need to feel connected to the past and the future, He calls on His people all throughout Scripture to constantly remember and rehearse their heritage—the story of their past. This is why He told the Israelites, "Remember the days of old; consider the generations long past. Ask your father and he will tell you, your elders, and they will explain to you.'" Deuteronomy 32:7, NIV

In fact, one of the reasons for the many ceremonies God required of Israel was so that future generations would learn the history and the unique calling of their people. For example, listen to God's instructions about the Passover, "Obey these instructions as a lasting ordinance for you and your descendants. When you enter the land that the Lord will give you as he promised, observe this ceremony. And when your children ask you, 'What does this ceremony mean to you?' then tell them, 'It is the Passover sacrifice to the Lord, who passed over the houses of the Israelites in Egypt and spared our homes when he struck down the Egyptians." Exodus 12:24–27, NIV

By celebrating the Feast of Passover each year, the Israelites embedded into the hearts of their children and grandchildren the understanding that God chose Israel and preserved her for His special purposes. Every young Israelite knew this almost from birth, and it powerfully shaped their lives.

Karl Marx once said, "A people without a heritage are easily persuaded." Without a heritage, people have little sense of destiny or purpose. They have a loose hold on the things that define their lives. But a people who have a heritage, particularly a godly heritage, have a strong sense of where they are going—in part because they recognize the flow of history which gives meaning and a sense of importance to their existence.

The effect that an awareness of one's own heritage and the sense of destiny this inspires is immense. Many magnificent things have been accomplished in history when people have understood their lives as a continuation of a divine purpose extending from generation to generation.

Consider the little known story of Stephen, an Italian sailor. In the 1400s, Stephen and a fellow sailor were walking an Algerian beach shortly before setting sail for their return to Italy. As they strolled the peaceful beach, they happened upon the battered body of a missionary to the Moslems who had been beaten and left for dead. Since they knew the missionary, they took him on board their ship and set sail, though a storm soon blew them off course. They ended up near the coast of Majorca, which happened to be the missionary's birthplace.

Aware that he was dying, the missionary asked to see the coast of Majorca once again. When he was brought on deck, though, he pointed not at his homeland but at the western horizon and said, "Beyond this sea that washes this continent we know, there lies another continent which we have never seen, whose natives are wholly ignorant of the Gospel. Send men there." Having spoken these words, he died.

Stephen returned to Italy and told this story to his children and then his grandchildren. One of Stephen's grandchildren took the story deeply to heart and sought God earnestly about the missionary's words. Soon this grandson recognized that Jesus had called him "to take the light of the Gospel to the heathen of undiscovered lands." And who was this grandson? Christopher . . . Christopher Columbus!

What is important about this story is how Christopher Columbus's life was shaped by a commission passed from generation to generation. The dying missionary's words formed part of the heritage that awakened a sense of destiny in Columbus's heart.

This is also how it is for us as Christians. We have a heritage that has been passed from generation to generation. At the heart of this heritage is God's commission to live for Him and to proclaim His kingdom to the entire world. As we learn about this great legacy and as we hear of the great men and women of God who are part of it, a sense of destiny is awakened in our hearts, just like what happened to Columbus. We sense a challenge to impact our generation with the power of God just as the great saints of old did in their own generation.

This is what the writer of the Psalms was describing when he wrote, "One generation will commend your works to another; they will tell of your mighty acts. They will speak of the glorious splendor of your majesty, and I will meditate on your wonderful works. They will tell of the power of your awesome works and I will proclaim your great deeds." Psalm 145:4–6, NIV

To See the Future

Another very important reason for learning about the past is to help us understand the future. The book of Ecclesiastes expresses this truth beautifully, "What has been will be again, what has been done will be done again; there is nothing new under the sun. Is there anything of which one can say, 'Look! This is something new? It was here already, long ago; it was here before our time.'" Ecclesiastes 1:9–10, NIV

"Whatever is has already been, and what will be has been before; and God will call the past to account." Ecclesiastes 3:15, NIV

Because God never changes and human nature is pretty much the same in every generation, we can be confident that things like those that happen today or tomorrow have already happened in the past. "What has been will be again." So, to study history is one of the best ways to understand the future, since history is, in a sense, going to be repeated in the future.

This is not the same thing, however, as saying that history goes in circles. In China, India, the Middle East, and the Greco-Roman worlds, people often thought of history as moving in great cycles—like a slowly rotating wheel.

This was largely for two reasons. First, the seasons of an individual's life from birth to maturity and then death were seen as the pattern for all of reality, including history. Secondly, the people who believed in cyclical time usually lived in a land where the yearly rhythm of the seasons determined much of the circumstances of their lives. It is not hard to imagine how they would see all of history in light of this cycle.

In the Christian view of history, though, time moves ever forward in a linear fashion while the experiences of men in history display reoccurring patterns. Again, this is because God doesn't change and human nature changes very little. So it sometimes seems, as Harry Truman said, that "the only thing new in the world is the history you don't know."

For example, it has taken modern man almost a century to discover whether communism would work or not. But those who knew history already had the answer. The Pilgrims tried socialized farming when they landed at Plymouth in 1620, and they almost starved. When they gave each family its own plot of land to work, the yield was many times larger than before. This and many other attempts at communism in the past revealed the future inefficiency and ultimate downfall of communism to those who knew history. The future had already been revealed in the past.

This is why so many of the great men and women who are known for showing inspired leadership in the face of an uncertain future have been devoted students of history. By understanding the past, they gained insight that helped them wisely answer the challenges of their day. As Winston Churchill, both a prize-winning historian and a great leader, once said, "The greatest advances in human civilization have come when we recovered what we had lost: when we learned the lessons of history."

Perhaps this is best expressed in Scripture when it is said of the men of the tribe of Issachar that they "understood the times" and "knew what Israel should do." 1 Chronicles 12:32, NIV

By first knowing their God and then understanding the background and realities of their own times, the men of Issachar had wisdom to direct Israel's future.

This is how Christians today can skillfully provide the leadership that will be needed for the battles ahead.

Escaping the "Kingdom of Now"

Author Richard Foster has written, "History has a wonderful way of freeing us from the cult of the contemporary." On the same theme, C. S. Lewis once wrote that to live lives of true depth and meaning, we must welcome "the fresh sea-breeze of the ages." What do these words mean?

If you've ever traveled to a foreign country, you may remember what it was like when you returned home. Because you had been to a land unlike your own, you saw things differently when you returned. You were more aware of the choices people were making, of the shape and pace of the things around you, and you understood the way your society is one option among many rather than the only way things can be.

This is also the way it can be when you visit the "far off country of the past." Studying history is like visiting a foreign land. You "travel" in this country called history and then you "return" to your own time. If you've really paid attention, you will see your own time differently because of what you've "seen" in the past. You'll realize how rich people are now or perhaps how sensual and comfort-oriented they are. Maybe you'll suddenly realize how fast-paced modern times are or you'll be thankful that women and people of non-white skin have so many freedoms. No matter what your response, you won't continue to be an unquestioning, unaware citizen of the "kingdom of now." You will, hopefully, live a richer, fuller, more meaningful life because you have "journeyed in time."

Cleansing the Land

Another insight that history offers a Christian is how the deeds of one generation can have an impact on a later generation. This is particularly true in matters of morality. The *Bible* speaks of this truth many times. Listen to 2 Samuel 21:1, NIV, "During the reign of David, there was a famine for three successive years; so David sought the face of the Lord. The Lord said, 'It is on account of Saul and his bloodstained house; it is because he put the Gibeonites to death.'"

According to the *Bible*, David's generation suffered because an earlier generation, Saul's generation, had committed murder.

Only when David addressed the wrongs of the past did his generation experience deliverance. In this case, the famine ended. This story illustrates one of the great truths of history: every generation is living in the wake of the generation that precedes it. This is not only how it is with moral and spiritual matters, but also with intellectual and even economic matters. We all live in the world that our ancestors have left us.

This means two things. First, we can't really understand our times unless we understand the past. Studying the present isn't enough because the past is always lurking just beneath the surface of the present. We have to understand how our history shapes us to understand who we really are.

It isn't enough just to understand the present. We also have to use insights into the past to change the present. In the same way that David summoned the Gibeonites and broke the famine by doing the right thing, we can also make reparations for wrong, repent of sins, stand against false philosophies, correct bad legislation, or do whatever is necessary to welcome the good and challenge the evils that our ancestors leave us. All of this is possible if we understand the moral, spiritual, intellectual, and social wake in which we live. Knowing history makes this possible.

The Cloud of Witnesses

In Hebrews 12:1, the *Bible* gives us a marvelous image for thinking about the past. After surveying the great men and women of the Old Testament in the eleventh chapter of

Hebrews, the author tells us that, "since we are surrounded by such a great cloud of witnesses" we should run the race that is set before our generation.

To understand this verse, you have to picture a track meet in a huge stadium. This is the picture that the original Greek language suggests. Up in the stands are the all the believers who have gone before us. We are surrounded by them—the way athletes on a field are surrounded by the crowds in the stands. They have all run their race, finished their course. Now it's our turn. In a sense, we have taken the baton from them, and we are now running the race God has set before our generation. But we have an advantage. We have the inspiration of their lives to spur us on to victory.

Certainly, this is one of the great benefits of knowing history. We are, in a sense, surrounded by great lives of old as we run the course chosen for us. Knowing their lives, what they had to overcome and endure, helps us to run well in our own generation.

Consider just a few of the amazing lives that have come before us.

A man was about to be burned at the stake for his faith in Jesus Christ, but even as the fire was lit and the flames lapped at his flesh, he kept on speaking of his Lord to the crowd of onlookers.

For sixty-six days a ship no larger than a volleyball court was tossed about in the frigid North Atlantic. The frequent storms were so violent that the passengers couldn't leave the lower decks for weeks at a time. But they endured all of it and more in the hope of becoming a "stepping-stone of the light of Christ" in the New World.

A Spanish missionary traveling in the North American wilderness was captured and horribly tortured by Indians. He escaped his captors and returned to his homeland. But later, he went back to live among the very Indians who had tortured him because he knew how desperately they needed Jesus Christ.

Stories like these from the lives of those who have faithfully served God in ages past have power to inspire and challenge us. This is one of the greatest blessings of history. To know how others have "fought the good fight" will light a fire of inspiration in our own lives.

Restoration

Okay, I admit it. I love Disney movies. I know, I know. I'm a sick man. But I love the lessons I can learn from even the simplest cartoon. I remember when I saw *The Lion King*. I walked around for days afterward saying, in my deepest Jamaican-sounding voice, "Remember who you are."

I love that line from the movie. I love it because I need to hear it. I often forget who I am. I forget who I'm called to be. I forget the good things that are part of my life and heritage. It helps me be better to hear someone say, even from a movie screen, "Remember who you are."

This is one of the things I get from knowing history. When I read about the past, I read how God empowered men and women to do astounding feats. He took orphans and wretches and made them noble. He took weaklings and cowards and made them conquerors. When I read these things, I realize as though for the first time what God wants to do in my life. I realize that God wants me to be more than what the *Bible* calls a "mere man." He wants me to conquer.

Think about it:

- God took a slave and made him a champion of his race—Booker T. Washington
- God took a cross-eyed waiter and made him the greatest preacher of his age—George Whitefield
- God took a sickly stutterer and made him the greatest leader of the twentieth century—Winston Churchill
- God took a depressed backwoodsman and made him the leader of his nation—Abraham Lincoln
- God took an illiterate Cherokee and used him to give his people an alphabet—Sequoia
- God took a failed clothing-store owner and made him the leader of his nation—Harry Truman

So when I read history, I remember what I'm called to be, what the possibilities are, and that something that I had lost can be restored. I read history now with the attitude that "I want it all." I want every good thing God has ever done through everybody I read about in history. My constant prayer is, "Restore what I've lost, O Lord. Restore what my generation has forgotten."

This is what history can do. It shouts to us from the ages, "Remember who you are."

Parachuting into the Past

A Survivor's Guide for Adventures in History

Suppose I gave you this assignment, "Parachute into a foreign country and find out what the people there believe. Find out what makes them tick and why they live the way they do. You have twenty-four hours." How would you fulfill this assignment? How would you quickly find out what is really at the core of that country, what really makes it what it is?

This is an important question for the study of history. Studying history really is like visiting a foreign country. In fact, some writers speak of "the far off country of the past." So I could ask you the same question about a time long ago as I could about a place far away. How would you find out what the people in the past believed and how those beliefs led them to live the way they did?

Since this is such an important part of learning about the past, let's look at some tools that will help you answer these questions. I would like to help you learn five simple definitions that will allow you to understand more clearly what makes any society tick—past or present. Armed with these definitions, all you'll need is your parachute!

What Is Religion?

When we think of religion, we normally think of churches, synagogues, mosques, symbols, priests, rituals, or denominations. These are all aspects of what we might call "formal religion," and this kind of religion does have a powerful impact upon human life.

But there is another, less formal kind of religion that really explains what men deem important—what they are willing to give their lives for or what occupies their thoughts, their checkbooks, or their calendars. Someone has suggested that this kind of religion is best described as "ultimate concern." A man's ultimate concern is what dominates his thoughts and passions, what he regards with unconditional seriousness, and what he is willing to suffer or die for. This is his religion, his god, his faith—regardless of what he says he believes.

For example, suppose a man says he's a Christian but his ultimate concern in life is pleasure. If pleasure is what motivates him, if pleasure is what he spends his money on and what fills his dreams, then pleasure is his religion. In the same way, another man might claim to be a Buddhist, and he may even be genuinely devoted to all of its practices. However, if his ultimate concern in life is success—if he devotes everything he has to achieving success—then success is his real religion.

This definition of religion can help us understand our society a little better. We often hear people say that we live in a non-religious society, but when we understand that religion is really ultimate concern, it becomes clear that we actually live in a very religious society. It is simply that our society is not religious in the traditional definition or sense of that word. There are many religions in our society: religions like sex, money, status, mankind, nature, and sometimes even the idea of religion itself. When any of these things become someone's ultimate concern, it becomes their religion.

But what does all this have to do with understanding history? When we look at the lives of people in history, we have to realize that each person's life has been shaped in large part by faith. Whatever people believed—their ultimate concern— was their religion, even if they claimed to be completely opposed to religion. A man may even have said he was an atheist, but he nevertheless used some kind of religion—his love of country, his passion for success, or even his love of reason, for example—to try to fill the spiritual void in his life.

So when we read history, we must try to understand how people's beliefs—meaning their ultimate concerns or religions—molded the lives they lived. Understanding people's faith is the key to understanding why they lived the way they did.

What Is Culture?

In the same way that we can see people's ultimate concerns exhibited in how they live, we can also see the ultimate concerns of an entire society displayed in what we call "culture." In fact, a good definition for culture is "religion externalized."

Think about what it is that really distinguishes Japanese culture or Spanish culture or American culture. Geography is part of the difference and so is biology, but the major distinctions are the fruits of the religions that permeate each society. This is what is meant when we say that culture is religion (ultimate concern) externalized.

Everything that we see when a society expresses itself is a representation of the aspirations, values, higher principles, and thought forms of people. Literature, architecture, philosophy, painting, dress, music, how people spend their time, what they think is "fair," the designs they prefer, the character of their leaders—these and all the other things which make up culture are reflections of a people's ultimate concerns or religions. This is as true for a society in the past as it is for societies today.

To show this more clearly, let's look at three important elements of culture: law, education, and art.

What Is Law?

A vital part of any society is law. When men make laws, they make a formal statement about what society considers important. For example, to outlaw murder is to say that human life is uniquely valuable. To pass laws that prohibit stealing is to make a statement about the priority of private property and personal freedom. Laws, all laws, are statements of value, of belief, of higher principles. This is why we might define law as "religion codified" or religion set into a series of statements about right and wrong.

Laws set the standards of behavior in a society. They establish what is considered fair and just, and they establish an order or a framework for people to live within. These things—justice, fairness, and order—can't be decided scientifically, since science can only deal with what is measurable, observable, and repeatable. But human behavior doesn't fit these categories. So men base their laws on what they believe is right—on the higher principles they believe are true for all men. This is clearly what religion is all about.

You will sometimes hear people say, "You can't legislate morality." This isn't true, though. In fact, morality is all you can legislate. For example, why don't we have laws that say all citizens must wear blue shirts on Tuesdays? Why don't we have laws that require pink flowers in all second-story window boxes? These laws sound silly, don't they? And the reason they sound silly is that they have nothing to do with morality, with right and wrong. That's why we have laws that deal with murder, stealing, personal assault, and discrimination. These are issues of truth, fairness—what is right. They are issues of religious truth.

This also explains why laws vary so widely between countries of the world. In some countries with an Islamic heritage, it is permissible to chop off the hand of a thief. This is because of the teaching of the Koran. In some countries, a woman has no rights to speak of and this is, again, because of the religious system that shapes the legal system. In Singapore it is illegal to chew gum . . . no kidding! This is because the laws were made according to the values of one man, and he didn't like the mess people made when they chewed gum! All of these laws sound strange to us because we have a different religious system behind our laws and a different understanding of what is true, what is right, and what is fair.

This is why, when you study history, you should pay attention to the importance of law. Understanding the laws of the societies you study can often tell you more about what the people really believe than anything else, even more than their formal statements of religion. Remember, law is the codification of the value system—the religion—of a people.

What Is Education?

When we say that a society's religion is codified in its laws, we should also add that its religion is also found in its schools. This is because when one generation teaches another, the older generation transmits to the next generation what it thinks is of ultimate importance for life. The older generation must have first answered the question, "What are the things our children need to know to live successfully?" Clearly, the answer to this question is a matter of faith, and that is why we can say that education is the transmission of religion to the next generation.

Consider this. A Christian will almost certainly say that for a school to really help its students to live a "successful life," it must teach salvation in Jesus Christ, a right fear of the Lord, and the study of all of reality as a creation of God. A humanist will say that a successful life requires self-respect and self-actualization, a complete freedom from the oppression of religion, and the full achievement of human potential. Schools, the humanist will insist, should impart these values. A Marxist, however, will say that the state should be the focus of all education, and that schools exist to shape students into useful workers and loyal supporters of world socialism.

Now, each of the above—the Christian, the humanist, and the Marxist—expect schools to transmit their values to the next generation. And they are each right, in a sense, because education is the transmission of what those doing the teaching think is of ultimate importance. Put another way, education is the transmission of religion from one generation to the next—in other words, "religion transferred."

So, when you study history or when you visit a foreign country, find out what is happening in the schools. Find out what the generation in charge is teaching the next generation. This will tell you more about what the people believe than all of their formal statements about religion and values.

What Is Art?

Art is such a vast and unwieldy subject that it is hard to think of a clear answer to the question, "What is art?" But even if we can't define all of what art is, perhaps we can define what art does. Art, some have suggested, is "religion symbolized."

Think about the different streams of art for a moment. There is the impressionist painter who shows us a starry night from his own very personal view. There is the rock and roll singer who appears on stage with hardly any clothes on and gyrates sensually to music that extols the joys of sex. And there is the photographer whose pictures depict a cross immersed in urine or two men kissing. What do each of these art forms have in common? The answer is that each is expressing an ultimate concern—our definition of religion. The ultimate concern of the painter is individualism and a subjective worldview. The ultimate concern of the rock and roll singer is pleasure and sensual fulfillment. And the ultimate concern of the photographer is personal freedom and hatred of any absolutes. Art is indeed religion symbolized.

Understanding this can give us insight into almost any society. For example, one of the ways that art is used in our own day is in advertising. We are constantly bombarded with advertising images, which are nothing more than art employed to inspire sales. The British author Norman Douglas once said, "You can tell the ideals of a nation by its advertisements." He was right, because advertising is little more than art (maybe not very high art!) supercharged to sell products.

When you sit in front of your television and watch the unending stream of commercials that pass before your eyes, you are getting a better representation of what is important to our society than you would sitting in Church or reading the great documents of our founding fathers. Advertisers work hard to understand what motivates people and then design ad campaigns that connect their product to the people's dreams and aspirations. But this is what all art does. It symbolizes what people hope, dream, and believe. In short, art symbolizes the ultimate concerns of a people.

So . . .

Armed with these definitions, you can cut right to the core of what people believe. So, here's what you do: listen to what they say, watch how they spend their money and their time, tap into their dreams and aspirations, and pay close attention to what they strive to achieve. Then you'll know what their religions are, and you can anticipate how those religions will shape all the elements of culture. In fact, you'll know more about what they believe and how they live than if you go into their churches or read their founding documents. Faith is what powers the human side of history. Find out what people believe and you'll know who they are.

Now, go get your parachute.

Doing History

Reading History and Living to Tell about It

Okay, we've rescued history from the evolutionary abyss. We've learned the four pillars of a Christian view of history. We've seen seven ways that history can change our lives. And we've packed away some tools for figuring out who people in the past or in the present really are. Now, let's "do" some history. Let's take what we've learned and keep it in our heads while we read about the past.

Now, wait a minute. Don't nod off. This could be fun. After all, I wrote this stuff!

Let's start with some fun themes in history. How about the movies? Almost everyone has heard of the movie Titanic. Let's join all the mania about this ship and use it to launch into a look at the *Titanic* story from a Christian perspective. And did you see the Disney movie Pocahontas? Well, let's use the real story behind the popular movie to dig up some little known Christian history.

How about some other themes? Surely you've heard of Winston Churchill. But did you know that the faith that made him great came first from a plump British nanny by the name of Elizabeth Everest? Hmmm. Might be interesting, huh? Then, we'll look at a revival in the early 1800s—a revival that changed our nation, and we'll look at how we are all living in the spiritual wake of the 1960s. Who knows. You might learn something. But maybe, just maybe, you may also get a glimpse of how history can be approached through the eye of faith. It could even be fun.

To help you a bit, I'll mention some things for you to think about at the beginning of each article. So, take your time. Relax. This book is almost finished! You're almost there. So, enjoy these last few pages and let your heart and your mind "do" some Christian history.

A Tale of Two Ships

This first article deals with the famous *Titanic* disaster. Now, if evolution is true, the *Titanic* sank because people were stupid and that's it. But if what we've been saying about a Christian view of history is true, then nothing happens without God having some purpose for it. So, in that light, what does the *Titanic* disaster mean? What does God want to say through the story of the *Titanic*? This is what a Christian historian (and that's what you're becoming, like it or not) has to ask about everything in history.

Now, with each of these articles, ask yourself how do the four pillars of a Christian view of history come into play? How does the story told in the article give an example of each pillar? Think about which of the seven benefits of history are most fulfilled in your life after reading the article. Ultimately, whenever you read history, you have to ask, "How will I live differently for what I've learned?" This is the "bottom line" of Christian history.

She was the largest ship in the world. In fact, she was the largest movable object man had ever made. Over eleven stories tall and almost a sixth of a mile long, she dwarfed the seaside buildings of Belfast where she first arose like a colossus and where her proud craftsmen took their grandchildren to view her beauty and contemplate her meaning in their lives.

Newspapers around the world took note of her and of her maiden voyage on that bright day from Southampton, England on April 10, 1912. She was, they said, "the promise and pride of a new age." And so she was. Her name was *Titanic*. Looking back, it is as though she was designed and outfitted to embody a century then still fresh and full of hope. She was born in an age still feigning innocence, before the first of two world wars, the economic follies of nations, and the confusing Babel of secular prophets left men cynical and unsure. Truly, she was inspiring. Her staterooms, ballrooms, restaurants, and fifty-foot-wide promenades were the talk of Europe. The loving attention lavished on her staircases, chandeliers, statuary, and paneled lounges is rivaled in memory only by that offered in the service of God by the builders of Christendom's great cathedrals. She shone with the best art, books, furniture, and even gold bathroom fixtures. She boasted a gym complete with exercise bikes, a rowing machine, a swimming pool, and a squash court. She even carried a Renault car, the finest hunting dogs available, four cases of opium, and luggage so expensive that one woman's alone was estimated at more than $177,000.

The *Titanic's* passengers were a cross-section of the age. From the largely Scots-Irish third class passengers making their way to new lives in America to the super rich who occupied luxurious berths in first class, those who boarded the liner on that hectic April day in Southampton were a microcosm of the world as it then was. Making their way onto the massive vessel was the richest man in the world, John Jacob Astor, and a

Frenchman who traveled with the children he had just kid-napped from the home of his estranged wife. Both the wealthy founder of Macy's department store, Isidor Straus, and a woman stealing west with her lover found their way onto the Titanic. Among the more than 2,200 passengers were million-aire playboy Ben Guggenheim, President Taft's military advisor, the music teacher to Theodore Roosevelt's children, a squash pro, a movie star, a thief, several gamblers, the Titanic's archi-tect, and hundreds of rather unremarkable, common people distinguished only by the dream that this glorious vessel would carry them to fortune. The *Titanic,* despite her name, was the world in miniature.

How significant it is, then, that as one frightened woman boarded the ship and nervously asked a nearby steward about its safety, the steward puffed out his chest and declared in a voice hundreds could hear, "Madam, God himself could not sink this ship." And how astonishing it is, now, that in that beautifully adorned ship's library, among the hundreds of books provided for leisure reading, there was one written by Morgan Robertson called *Futility*. Not significant at first, per-haps, except that it told the fictional story of a ship called Titan, which struck an iceberg and sank at sea with huge loss of life. Futility was written in 1898—fourteen years before the Titanic's only voyage. No one had checked out the book; no one heard the warning.

So on the evening of the third day of the voyage, when through the cold, crystalline, night air the lookout's warning bell sounded, the people of the *Titanic*—in all their variety and comfort and hope—were behaving in a way that is only notable because it was so incredibly and tragically . . . normal. But the deathblow had already occurred. Seconds before lookout Frederick Fleet—whose position was called "the eyes of the ship"—had reported, "Iceberg right ahead." The Titanic, whose captain had been ignoring ice warnings from other ships for three days, now attempted an evasive maneuver. The First Mate cut the ship's speed and called for a turn hard to port. With only thirty-seven seconds between first sighting and impact, the officer's efforts were futile at best and may have made matters worse. At 11:40PM on April 14, Titanic collided with an iceberg on her starboard side leaving a gash twelve square feet in size. The ship was doomed. Most passengers thought the wind had picked up a bit, nothing more.

The ship was unsinkable. So there were only lifeboats for 1,178 of the 2,207 passengers. Ships that God can't sink don't need lifeboats. As the shrill alarms sounded throughout the warm, sleepy ship and women and children began boarding the chilly lifeboats along with the men grumbling about the inconvenience of this "drill," the cruel reality settled into the mind first of the captain and then his crew—hundreds of people were going to die. There simply were not enough lifeboats. Probably more than one crewman remembered that the reason there were twenty rather than the needed forty-eight lifeboats was to make space for those fifty-foot-wide promenades so loved by the stylishly clad strollers of first class.

Panic soon set in. Half-empty lifeboats were launched into the oil-black sea. Men posed as women and left their friends behind to save their own lives. Crewmen used pistols to enforce order. In the first class lounge, drunken card games continued undisturbed by the general chaos. Passengers in third class were locked below decks until the upper classes had boarded the boats. Husbands lied to their wives and children to get them into the boats against their protests, and men silently prepared themselves in semi-shock for their icy end.

At 2:20AM on Sunday, April 15, the ship, which had been slowly sinking nose down, suddenly groaned and lifted her twenty-three-foot propellers high into the air as she slid into her black grave, exploding into halves from the weight of her own steel before plummeting more than two miles to the bottom of the ocean. Some fifteen hundred passengers—half of whom could have found space in the half-filled lifeboats and all of whom should have been saved had the ship not been arrogantly deemed "unsinkable" and denied the right number of boats—plunged into the bitter-black chill of the North Atlantic.

Moments later, as shivering survivors balanced upon an upturned, collapsible lifeboat, someone suggested that it might be appropriate to pray. There was discussion. Disagreement. Agreement. Then, together, they prayed the Lord's Prayer. Finally.

News of the sinking and the few survivors, of the agony and loss, sped throughout the world. Preachers immediately seized upon the theme of pride and arrogance, calling for national and even international repentance. The *Atlantic Constitution* saw another lesson. Its editors claimed that the behavior of gentlemen in *Titanic's* first class confirmed that "the Anglo-Saxon may yet boast that his sons are fit to rule the earth." In reply, black folk-singer Leadbelly offered these lyrics: "Black man oughta shout for joy; Never lost a girl or either a boy." Lookout Frederick Fleet, ironically the first to see the iceberg and yet one of the survivors, complained loudly that the ship might have been saved if, in the midst of excess and opulence, the "eyes of the ship" had been granted the oft-requested but oft-denied binoculars. The reason for the denial, he explained bitterly to the astonished world press, was that binoculars were deemed a "frivolous expense." For such audacity, fellow survivors, claiming betrayal, ostracized Frederick Fleet for the rest of his life.

The much-debated prophecy of the *Titanic* haunts men today more than at any time since the horrors of that Atlantic night. The ship's tale has been the theme of an award-winning Broadway play. Her story has been depicted in one of the most expensive movies ever made. In addition, she has been the subject of computer games, best-selling books, and thousands of Internet web sites. The best-selling book on the *Titanic*, hauntingly entitled, *A Night to Remember,* has not gone out of print since its first appearance in 1955. The Titanic holds aloft the fear and arrogance and vanity and folly that defines all societies in decline, and clearly we fear, or perhaps we know, that the Titanic story is that of our own age, and now, perhaps, its fate.

But there was another ship.

This second ship left from the same Southampton port, though she departed almost 400 years before the *Titanic*. She, too, traversed the frigid North Atlantic. She, too, bore passengers and their dreams. Yet, there the similarities end. This second ship was a far humbler offering. No larger than a volleyball court and but a few stories high—she would have fit completely inside one of *Titanic's* ornate ballrooms—she leaked profusely. Moreover, she held only 105 passengers and crew and offered relatively little space for supplies in her hold. The whole idea, in fact, of sailing to "the northern parts of Virginia" at such a time of year with such a crew and in such a ship was a fool's fancy. Who would even dare such a thing?

But this second ship, after sixty-six wintry days on the violent North Atlantic, reached safe harbor. She shouldn't have. Halfway across the ocean the ship was slammed by such a violent storm that the main beam broke. Surely all 105 aboard would die a cruel, icy death at sea. Then one among them remembered the printing press on board with its giant screw. Using the screw as a jack, the crew pressed the main beam back into place. A miracle. And there was more. Violent storms forced the passengers below deck with hatches bolted for weeks at a time. There was a death at sea. Many were severely ill. There were pregnant women on board. Perhaps worse, more than one third of the passengers were children. It was a terrifying, vomiting, bone-breaking experience of sixty-six days. They should never have made it.

Yet, when they did finally arrive, they announced to the world both who they were and their reason for sailing. They had voyaged, they wrote, "for the glory of God and the advancement of the Christian faith." They wanted to be "but stepping stones of the light of Jesus" that the natives of this land might "embrace the Prince of Peace" and that a new "land of light" might be a resting-place for "the glory of God." They called their proclamation the "Mayflower Compact"—named for their cramped, little ship. Themselves they called Pilgrims, "strangers in a strange land," who in "this howling wilderness of the New World" could be sustained but "by the Spirit of God and his grace."

This is the tale of two ships. One, proudly named, proudly outfitted, and proudly sailed to the glory of a new age as testimony of the genius of man. The other, with no natural hope of success, launched to the glory of God by his humble servants for the benefit of generations yet unborn. The first, after three days of ease, sinks. The second, after sixty-six days of hell, arrives safely. The first does not heed the warnings, does not read the signs, does not even know it is sinking. The second sails because it knows the signs of the times and seeks to answer its dangers with the power of a different kingdom. The name of the first is a symbol of decadent destruction. The power of the second launched a nation. This is the age-old distinction, the eternal chasm, between the City of God and the City of Man, between the Prince of Pride and the Suffering Servant made Lord. It is the story of mankind, the ultimate question of destiny. It is the tale of two ships.

Pocahontas: The Real Story

One of the things you quickly realize when you start reading history from a Christian perspective is that the truth is often hidden beneath a layer of myth. Christian historians often have to unearth the true story from the secular myths that hide the faith. This is what happened with the story of Pocahontas. Even before the Disney film, there were so many myths about this Indian princess you could hardly figure out who she was. The movie only made it worse. However, the true story that a little research reveals is actually a very inspiring one.

So, think about how the true story differs from what you have learned. Why do you suppose the myths that obscured the true story are so widely held? Remember to think about the four pillars of Christian history and the seven benefits. Ask yourself which ones are really highlighted by this story. You might also use your definitions of religion to analyze the two religions that come into contact in the world of the real Pocahontas.

According to the Disney version of her story, Pocahontas was a beautiful and quite shapely Indian woman who, not wanting to marry the man of her father's choosing, instead fell in love with the Englishman John Smith, saved his life at the risk of her own, and prevented a war between the white men and the Powhatan Indian tribe. Told with the familiar Disney flair, this makes for an enthralling children's cartoon; but none of it is true.

The movie also portrays Pocahontas talking to a spirit that lives in a tree, believing that all things, "the earth, the water, the sky," have spirits, and learning to listen to these spirits as they guide her life. This part is true. What the movie does not portray, though, is how Pocahontas later became a Christian and inspired all of England to carry the Gospel to the New World—a tale we ought now to recover and impress on the hearts of our children.

When the three ships that carried the Jamestown colonists landed on the banks of the James River in 1607, Pocahontas was a twelve or thirteen-year-old Indian princess. Her people called her Matoaka, which means wanton or lively. This may say a great deal about her energy and character. Her father was the powerful chieftain Powhatan, who ruled an empire spanning most of the eastern seaboard.

To the newly landed Englishmen, Matoaka's tribe must have seemed a strange and violent people. The men wore the right sides of their heads shaved while the left side grew long. Both men and women had three large holes in each ear into which some warriors inserted live snakes or dead animals. A bird's feather or the dried hand of an enemy might provide the headdress, but this latter adornment was taken only after the enemy was quartered, flayed alive, and then burned. The almost 9,000 people of the Powhatan empire worshipped harsh and demanding spirits that controlled all of life and to dishonor them meant certain destruction. As the gods of the

Powhatan dealt with their subjects, so the Powhatan dealt with their enemies.

So much of the story of the Englishmen at Jamestown has centered around John Smith. Even today a heroic statue of the Captain stands near the site of the original settlement along the James River commemorating his leadership of the colony. The facts paint a different story. Smith arrived in Virginia as a prisoner. He had been arrested under suspicion of conspiring to seize control of the colony. Smith's fellow colonists angrily built a gallows on which to hang him during a stopover at Nevis Island, but reason prevailed. Not until their arrival in the New World did Smith seem of any value at all. Only when the laziness and ill planning of the Jamestown colonists nearly led to their starvation, did Smith's years of experience as a soldier in the Turkish wars, as a slave of Crimean Tartars, and, yes, even as a pirate, begin to prove useful. He seemed to understand the Indians and knew how to barter for food with trinkets. For this skill and his proclaiming himself the "President of Virginia," when the ruling council scampered back to England, Smith has been called the "Savior of Jamestown."

The reality is that Smith left Jamestown in 1609, only two years after the colony was founded and when its future was still very much in question. And what of the famous story of Pocahontas saving Smith's life by placing her head upon his? It probably isn't true. During the years Smith was in Jamestown he kept a journal, which he later published as *A True Relation of Virginia Since the First Planting of that Colony*. In it, he says nothing about his life being saved by Pocahontas, who could have been no more than fourteen years old at the time. Instead, the only source for the story comes from a book Smith wrote some fifteen years after he left Jamestown, entitled *A Generall Historie of Virginia, New-England, and the Summer Isles.* Smith was such a swaggering glory-hound that most historians believe he fabricated the story to add to the romance of his adventures. The likelihood that a fourteen-year-old Indian princess would defy her father the King and place her head on the block to save an invader of her people is too much to believe.

Yet, one thing Smith said may well be true. In his journal he wrote that Pocahontas was as "next under God . . . the instrument to preserve this colony from death, famine, and utter confusion." Though Smith was almost certainly referring to her saving his life, the truth is that God did use Pocahontas, not only to save the colony but also to bring the gospel to her people. She was indeed an instrument of God.

On April 13, 1613, years after John Smith had left the colony and during a time of great tension between the Englishmen and their Indian neighbors, Pocahontas was taken prisoner and held hostage within the fort at Jamestown. She had not visited the English since the days of John Smith, and it was evident to all that she had grown into a stunning woman, now of eighteen or nineteen years. For over a year she was held hostage, and during that time an enterprising planter by the name of John Rolfe fell madly in love with the princess. But what should he do? There was no precedent for such a thing—a marriage between an Indian and an Englishman—and

Rolfe was sure it would be frowned upon. Yet, encouraged by her warmth and receptivity to his love, Rolfe wrote a letter requesting that his leaders give permission for him to marry the girl.

"My chiefest intent and purpose be . . . to strive with all my power of body and mind in the undertaking of so mighty a matter—in no way led with the unbridled desire of carnal affection, but striving for the good of this plantation, for the honor of our country, for the Glory of God and Jesus Christ of an unbelieving creature, namely Pocahontas, to whom my hearty and best thoughts are, and have for a long time been so entangled and enthralled in so delicate a labyrinth . . . Almighty God, who never faileth His who truly invoke His Holy Name, hath opened the gate."

Both the leaders of Jamestown and Powhatan himself were bemused at the prospect and gave their consent. The impending wedding was like a sunburst of light that warmed the dangerous chill in the relations between the two nations. But there was one problem. Rolfe could not marry a non-believer; he could not be unequally yoked. To remedy the problem, the Rev. Alexander Whitaker was enlisted to teach Pocahontas not only the truth of the Gospel of Jesus but also the English language. And, as one eminent historian has written, "She took readily to both and soon renounced idolatry, openly confessed her Christian faith, and, 'as she desired,' was baptized Rebecca." On April 5, 1614, John and Rebecca Rolfe were married in the timber Church of Jamestown with Powhatan and his court in attendance.

The marriage transformed the relations between the Indians and the white men. Hostilities ended for many years. Food, tools, and culture were exchanged, and some of the Indians even followed Rebecca in giving their lives to Jesus. Then an even greater opportunity arose for Rebecca to serve her newfound Lord. In May of 1616, John Rolfe, who had developed a type of tobacco that was becoming quite popular in England, was invited to return to his homeland. Rebecca went with her husband along with ten or twelve Indians. Upon their arrival in England, Mistress Rolfe charmed London society both with her command of the English language and her devotion to Jesus. She met with the bishop of London, with lords and ladies, and even with royalty. And in each of these meetings she spoke of her conversion, of her joy, and of her people's need for the gospel of Jesus. As the Rev. Samuel Purchas later wrote, Rebecca "carried her self as the Daughter of a King, and was accordingly respected, not only by the [Virginia] Company but of divers persons of Honor in their hopeful zeal by her to advance Christianity." England captured a fresh vision from Rebecca—a vision of the power of the Gospel in the New World.

The trip was a huge success. John Rolfe's planting skills were promising to pay well in England, Rebecca had become a favorite at Court, and the leaders of the Church of England had promised that many missionaries would be sent to the people of the New World. And then, with all of this hope and promise in her heart, while she was waiting for the tides that would carry her home, Rebecca contracted a disease, probably tuberculosis, and died at Gravesend on March 21, 1617. She was buried there in the parish Church. All England mourned her.

It is interesting that what most Americans "know" of the woman who was Pocahontas and who became Rebecca is false. They don't know the wonderful truth of her life. She was a princess in a wild and spiritually dark land. She fell in love with a young Englishman. To become one with the man she loved she had to become one with his Lord, which she did, passionately and openly. She grew rapidly in her new faith, and when her husband's prosperity gave her the opportunity, she astonished English society with the passion of her faith and a heart-cry for her people to know her Jesus. Though she died before she could return to her homeland, she had planted an all-important seed in the hearts of hundreds of Englishmen. "A New World awaits, and the people there need Jesus. Come, and disciple my people."

Given how Indian/white relations unfolded in the following centuries, Rebecca stands as a glorious symbol of what might have been. European Christians from Columbus to the Pilgrims had looked to the New World with a hunger from God to lead the Indians to Jesus. But at Jamestown, a young girl—a Princess, no less—had fallen in love, had given her heart to Jesus, and had become one in Christian marriage with a white man. What might that marriage between a Christian Indian and a Christian Englishman have meant? What power was in it and what a statement it was of the destiny and true purpose of this nation. That Christians were called from afar to proclaim Jesus to an unsaved people and become one with them in heart and faith is without question. That greed and hatred caused this commission to be laid aside is also without question. But perhaps the greatest hope for a restoration of that commission, and of this nation's destiny, is that stories such as that of Rebecca be remembered and passed down from generation to generation. For, as Psalm 88:12 asks, "Can righteousness be done in a land of forgetfulness?"

The Hidden Calling

Because there is a God, small actions can have great impact. Common people can live exceptional lives. This is true of the lady you're going to read about now. She was just a simple nanny, but she changed the world.

Remember to think about what we've learned. Particularly think about how God uses people who don't even know they're a crucial part of His plan. He can do this because He is a sovereign God. It might be especially helpful to look at Winston Churchill's life in light of the spiritual battles that have shaped history. How was Elizabeth Everest used to fight those battles? Don't forget to think about how this story impacts your own life and how you can live differently in light of what this article has taught you. Remember that's what Christian history is all about.

Her name was Elizabeth Anne Everest. Few today will remember her. In fact, few would have known of her even during her lifetime, which ended in near obscurity in 1895. She was, after all, only a nanny—one of thousands in Victorian England—who quietly spent their days caring for the children of other people. Strolling in a park with the baby's carriage or braving the London streets with a little boy clinging tightly to her side, there would have been nothing to distinguish her to passersby. She was just another British nanny with another nobleman's son in her charge.

Or so it would seem. But Elizabeth Anne Everest was not just another nanny. She was a Christian of the most passionate and fearless kind. For her, being a nanny was not just a job, it was a ministry. She lived her faith boldly before the families that hired her and worked hard to build godliness and biblical truth into the young lives in her care. Thus it was, while serving her Lord in the hiddenness of her calling, that she came to have an impact upon the course of modern history. For on a blustery English day in February of 1875, Elizabeth Everest came to be the nanny, and soon the primary spiritual influence, of one rosy-cheeked baby boy by the name of Winston Leonard Spencer Churchill, future Prime Minister of England and leader of the western world.

There was little hint in his early years, however, of the greatness that young Winston would one day command, and Mrs. Everest soon understood the immensity of her task. In time, the boy's mother would warn visitors, with typical British understatement, that he was "a difficult child to manage." She was right. He kicked, he screamed, he hid, and he bullied. The word "monster" was often used of him, and the trouble was that he was bright, too. Knowing of Mrs. Everest's Christian faith, young Winston once tried to escape a mathematics lesson by threatening to "bow down and worship graven images." It worked, too . . . for a while. But Elizabeth Everest was an exceptional woman. She knew how to enforce the boundaries she set, and from the beginning Winston held a grudging respect for this woman who seemed to know the secret—that his irritating behavior only served to hide the desperate longing of his heart.

This was the truth she tenderly guarded, for she knew that her Lord had not entrusted young Winston to her solely for the discipline she would enforce but more for the vacuum she would fill in the life of this lonely little boy. Few knew how painful his loneliness really was. It would be nice, indeed, to report that the Churchills shared a warmly intimate home life and that Winston was smothered with parental affection, but nothing could be farther from the truth. Quite to the neglect of their son, Randolph and Jennie Churchill gave themselves completely to their social ambitions. True, Victorian parents maintained an astonishing distance from their children, receiving them only at prearranged times and under the watchful eye of servants, but the Churchills were remote even by these standards. Of his mother, Winston later wrote, "I loved her, but at a distance." His father thought Winston was retarded, rarely talked to him, and regularly vented his mounting rage on the child. More than one historian has concluded that Lord Randolph simply loathed his son.

Thus it was that Elizabeth Everest—Winston came to call her "Woom"—became not only his nanny but his dearest companion, sharing with understanding and tender loyalty the secrets of his widening world. She was, after all, the stereotypical British nanny—plump, simple, cheery, ever optimistic, always compassionate. The boy grew to love her completely. Of their special relationship, Violet Asquith later wrote that in Winston's "solitary childhood and unhappy school days Mrs. Everest was his comforter, his strength and stay, his one source of unfailing human understanding. She was the fireside at which he dried his tears and warmed his heart. She was the night light by his bed. She was security."

She was also his shepherd, for it was here, in the safety of their shared devotion, that Winston first experienced genuine Christianity. On bended knee beside this gentle woman of God he first learned that surging of the heart called prayer. From her lips he first heard the Scriptures read with loving devotion and was so moved he eagerly memorized his favorite passages. On long walks together they sang the great hymns of the Church, spoke breathlessly of the heroes of the faith, and imagined aloud what Jesus might look like or how heaven would be. As they sat together on a park bench or on a blanket of cool, green grass, Winston was often transfixed while Woom explained the world to him in simple but distinctly Christian terms. And it is not hard to imagine that when their day was done, many an evening found this devoted intercessor praying the prayers of destiny over her sleeping charge, asking her Heavenly Father to fulfill the calling she sensed so powerfully on his life.

It would seem her prayers were answered, for though in early adulthood Churchill immersed himself in the anti-Christian rationalism that swept his age, he eventually recovered his faith during an escape from a South African prison. So deeply had he received the imprint of Mrs. Everest's dynamic faith that in this time of crisis the prayers he had learned at her knee returned almost involuntarily to his lips, as did the Scripture passages he had memorized to the familiar lilt of her voice. From that time forward, his faith defined him, as it did his sense of mission. He came to see himself in much the same terms as those he once used to dedicate his grandson. Holding the child aloft, he tearfully proclaimed him "Christ's new faithful soldier and servant."

So when the tests of life had prepared him, and his day of destiny arrived, Winston Churchill was ready to lead the world with a clear trumpet call of the solid faith he first learned from his godly nanny. In an age of mounting skepticism, Church proclaimed the cause of "Christian civilization." It was threatened from without, he believed, by "barbarous paganism"—like Nazism—which spurned "Christian ethics" and derived its "strength and perverted pleasure from persecution." Therefore, every Christian had a "duty to preserve the structure of humane, enlightened, Christian society." This was critical, he believed, for "once the downward steps are taken, once one's moral intellectual feet slipped upon the slope of plausible indulgence, there would be found no halting-place short of a general Paganism and Hedonism."

While other leaders of his age vacillated and sought the compromises of cowards, Churchill defined the challenges of his civilization in the stark Christian terms that moved men to greatness. Yet behind the arsenal of his words, behind the artillery of his vision, was the simple teaching of a devoted nanny who served her God by investing in the destiny of a troubled boy.

So it was that when the man some called the "Greatest Man of the Age" lay dying in 1965 at the age of ninety, there was but one picture that stood at his bedside. It was the picture of his beloved nanny, who had gone to be with her Lord some seventy years before. She had understood him, she had prayed him to his best, and she had fueled the faith that fed the destiny of nations . . . in the hiddenness of her calling.

Fire in the West: The Logan County Revivals

As we've seen, God rules history. Sometimes He uses Elizabeth Everests to shape destiny and sometimes He uses great mass movements and revivals. The revival called the Second Great Awakening permanently changed American history, and the story you're about to read tells of the beginning of that great outpouring of God's Spirit.

As you read, think about how the conditions of society before the revival mirror your own time. How did those conditions change? What kind of people did God use? Remember, one of the reasons we study the past is to find solutions for the present. What solutions for your generation do you see in this story? Don't forget the big question! How will you live differently for what you've learned?

When the earliest English settlers came to the New World, they did so "for the glory of God and the advancement of the Christian faith." In a solemn covenant, they asked God to make them a "stepping stone of the light of Christ" for the purpose of founding a Christian nation. And once they arrived as strangers in this strange land, their enduring prayer was that God would keep their descendants faithful to Him, restoring them in mercy should they stray.

These early prayers and covenants may well explain the pattern of decline and revival so clearly evident in American history. True, national revivals can be found in many nations throughout Church history. But revivals in this country have normally arrived at such strategic moments of heart-rending spiritual decline and included such unique themes of restoration and destiny, that it is not hard to imagine a covenant-keeping God responding even still to the prayers of Pilgrim and Puritan forebearers.

Faith in Crisis

Few revivals reflect this more than the one which God mercifully granted in the late 1790s, the one now called the Second Great Awakening. By this date, the United States should have been a rising Christian republic. After all, the War for Independence had just been won against a king whom many colonists believed to be "the Antichrist." A new Constitution and Bill of Rights gave promise of both political stability and complete religious freedom, and most Americans thought of themselves as Christians in a Christian nation.

The reality, however, was that a uniquely American brand of civil religion had crept in, subtly replacing biblical Christianity with faith in the nation itself. And under cover of this creeping idolatry, a radically anti-Christian philosophy began to take root. If a newspaper of the more recent breed had summarized this crisis of faith in the familiar "At-a-Glance" fashion, it might have looked something like this:

- Established denominations fail to recover from destruction of War. Property and clergy loss profound.

- Only ten percent of population now attends Church.
- Thomas Paine and Ethan Allen, made household names during War years, now espouse anti-Christian deism and Enlightenment philosophy.
- Paine's *Age of Reason* calls Christianity a "fable," the book of Genesis an "invented absurdity." Thomas Paine Societies abound nationwide.
- Rise of Unitarian President, Thomas Jefferson, prompts concern among conservative clergy.
- National spirit of independence prevails, feeds resistance to traditional "faith of the Fathers."

Of course, no such article would have been complete without quotes from "alarmed religious leaders."

- Episcopalian Rector Devereaux Jarratt says "religion at low ebb," "situation gloomy and truly suspicious and discouraging."
- The Baptists are "declining . . . the Methodists are splitting and falling to pieces."
- Presbyterian Synod of Virginia reports "vice and wickedness in some of their most insulting and infamous forms abound in our Country."
- Brethren missionaries conclude "especially among upper classes, deism and irreligion rule beyond all bounds."
- Lack of "praying ministry" decried by itinerant Methodists.

Without question, the land was in the grip of evil—any hope of a Christian future clearly imperiled. And nowhere did it seem as bad as in that region of southern Kentucky called Logan County. While visiting the area, Methodist Bishop Francis Asbury had written in 1797, "When I reflect that not one in a hundred came here to get religion, but rather to get plenty of good land, I think it will be well if some or many do not eventually lose their souls?" The bishop was more right than he knew. This virtually lawless region had become a habitation for so many "murderers, horse thieves, highway robbers, and counterfeiters" that the criminals themselves renamed the district "Rogue's Harbor." Methodist circuit rider Peter Cartwright, who grew up in Logan County, wrote that the people represented a "desperate state of society" filled with violence and outrage.

Indeed, so legendary had the wickedness and corruption of the county become that the virtuous citizens formed themselves into "Regulators" and attempted to enforce a makeshift law code. The quarrel between the "Rogues and the Regulators" grew heated to the point of violence, and many on both sides were killed. Eventually, though the Regulators hunted and lynched many of the criminals, the Rogues rallied in strength and the Regulators fled. Cartwright wrote that when news of the bloodshed reached the nation it was "to the great scandal of civilized people."

The Fire of James McCready

Into this bedeviled territory rode James McCready on a warm day in 1796. McCready was a Scots-Irish Presbyterian, though not of the traditional variety. He wore buckskin breeches and spoke with rough plainness of a pioneer that other frontiersmen found appealing. He was born in Pennsylvania but moved to North Carolina while a young child. McCready himself said that he "never omitted prayer from the time he was seven, did not drink, swear, break the Sabbath, or indulge in other excesses." In 1788, when he was about thirty years old, he was licensed by the presbytery of Redstone in Pennsylvania and soon found himself ministering in Guilford County, North Carolina.

When McCready arrived in the Carolinas, he found that Christianity was in a sad condition. Before long, though, his stirring preaching about the wrath of God ignited revival fires, and many in the area were converted. One of McCready's converts was Barton W. Stone, who would later lead the famous Cain Ridge Revival in Bourbon County, Kentucky. Stone wrote of McCready:

"His person was not prepossessing, nor his appearance interesting, except his remarkable gravity and small, piercing eyes. His coarse, tremulous voice excited in me the idea of something unearthly. His gestures were *sui generis*, the perfect reverse of elegance. Everything appeared by him forgotten but the salvation of souls. Such earnestness, such zeal, such powerful persuasion . . . I had never before witnessed."

McCready's ministry in South Carolina, though, was not as well received as in North Carolina. He was accused of "running people distracted" and of keeping people from their labors and duties. At one point, protesters tore out his pulpit and burned it. When a letter written in blood warned McCready that his future was not bright in the state, he decided to accept the invitation of several friends to move west into the southern part of Kentucky.

Plowing the Ground

When McCready entered Logan County, amazingly even the Rogues regarded this man of rough appearance as one of their own. In January of 1797, in the manner of frontier society, McCready became the pastor of three churches, one at Red River, one at Gasper River, and one at Muddy River. Before long it became clear that the vision of this tall, heavy-set preacher was no less than to see Logan County transformed by a mighty work of God's Spirit. People were astounded, for many who had attempted similar success were driven out or even killed. However, McCready had walked this road before and, unlike his experience in South Carolina, he would not be moved.

McCready immediately began the fiery preaching and diligent pastoral efforts which had brought success in North Carolina. Though "universal deadness and stupidity" prevailed for a season, the darkness began to lift a bit with eight or nine people claiming conversion. By the next winter, though, the old deadness returned and many fell away. McCready was determined, though, and he had a secret weapon—a solemn Covenant of Prayer. Those who were willing were asked to sign it and give themselves to it wholeheartedly. It was the kind of statement which drew the proverbial line in the sand.

"When we consider the word and promises of a compassionate God, to the poor lost family of Adam, we find the strongest encouragement for Christians to pray in faith—to ask in the name of Jesus for the conversion of their fellowmen. None ever went to Christ, when on earth, with the case of their friends that were denied, and although the days of his humiliation are ended, yet for the encouragement of his people, he has left it on record, that when two or three agree upon earth, to ask in prayer, believing it shall be done. Again, whatsoever ye shall ask the Father in my name that will I do, that the Father may be glorified in the Son. With these promises before us we feel encouraged to unite our supplications to a prayer-hearing God, for the out-pouring of his Spirit, that his people may be quickened and comforted, and that our children, and sinners generally, may be converted.

"Therefore we bind ourselves to observe the third Saturday of each month, for one year, as a day of fasting and prayer, for the conversion of sinners in Logan County, and throughout the world. We also engage to spend one-half hour every Saturday evening, beginning at the setting of the sun, and one-half hour every Sabbath morning, at the rising of the sun, in pleading with God to revive his work."

For more than six months nothing happened. In fact, things got worse. The valiant band of prayer warriors searched their hearts and repented of their own sins. And then it happened. On the fourth Sunday of July, 1798, during a "sacramental meeting" of the Gasper River congregation, "the Lord poured out his Spirit in a very remarkable manner." Many were "gloriously awakened" and the fires began to spread. By the first Sunday of September, the people of Muddy River were similarly moved, and then it hit the Red River congregation. It seemed that the satanic hold on Logan County was about to be broken as increasing numbers reported marvelous "proofs" of God's Spirit.

Yet, as they always have during mighty moves of God, detractors arose. Presbyterian minister James Balch arrived almost as soon as the awakening began and so ridiculed the entire revival with its emotionalism and seeming excesses that confusion set in. Balch's attacks lasted for almost a year and when he was done, McCready sadly reported that his three congregations lay in "a dismal state of deadness and darkness."

He was not about to give up, though. He had tasted revival and knew it was worth any price. He earnestly fasted and prayed and called others to do the same. God honored their humility before him, for as McCready wrote, ". . . a remarkable spirit of prayer and supplication was given to Christians, and a sensible, heart-felt burden of the dreadful state of sinners out of Christ: so that it might be said with propriety, that Zion travailed in birth to bring forth her spiritual children."

Slowly, the tide began to turn. One congregation after another experienced the moving of God's Spirit. There was even a new Church founded at Clay-lick and revival swept that congregation as well. At Muddy River, in late September of 1799, "the greatest and most solemn and powerful time of any that had been before" occurred. The congregations swelled, and many were convinced that the long-sought revival had begun. The promise of a greater work during the sacramental meetings of the next summer kept the covenanted intercessors praying throughout the winter, though some of the converted lapsed into complacency. McCready was confident that the first breakings of a mighty work of God had taken place. Of what would happen that next summer, he later wrote:

"All the blessed displays of Almighty power and grace, all the sweet gales of the divine Spirit, and soul-reviving showers of the blessings of Heaven which we enjoyed before, and which we considered wonderful beyond conception; were but like a few scattering drops before a mighty rain, when compared with the overflowing floods of salvation, which the eternal, gracious Jehovah has poured out like a mighty river, upon this our guilty, unworthy country. The Lord has indeed shewed himself a prayer-hearing God: he has given his people a praying spirit and a lively faith, and then he has answered their prayers far beyond their highest expectations."

Like a Mighty River

In June of 1800, four or five hundred members of the three congregations met at Red River meeting house for a series of services scheduled to last from Friday to Monday. For many in attendance, this was the third year they had been praying for revival. Expectation ran high. For the first few days of the meetings, people were touched repeatedly. But on the last service of the last day, the dam broke.

William Hodge, a minister who had joined McCready, preached a long and powerful sermon. People began to weep, and one woman in the east end of the building began to cry and shout. When Hodge was through, it was Methodist preacher John McGee's turn. McGee began to sense the power of what God was doing and he later said, "there was one greater than I preaching." He continued his sermon.

"I exhorted them to let the Lord Omnipotent reign in their hearts and submit to Him, and their souls should live. Many broke silence. The woman in the east end of the house shouted tremendously. I left the pulpit to go to her . . . Several spoke to me: 'You know these people. Presbyterians are much for order, they will not bear this confusion.' I turned to go back—and was near falling, the power of God was strong upon me. I turned again and losing sight of fear of man, I went through the house exhorting with all possible ecstasy and energy."

The power of the Spirit was overwhelming. McCready observed that the floor was "covered with the slain; their screams for mercy pierced the heavens." One could see "profane swearers and Sabbath-breakers pricked to the heart and crying out 'What shall we do to be saved?'"

When the meeting was over, the ministers were dumbfounded but they were sure that the Lord was working. Plans were made immediately to hold another sacramental service at the Gasper River Church the last weekend in July. McCready believed that news of the Red River event would give hope to the neighboring congregations, and he worked hard to spread the news. He also realized the potential that huge crowds may attend. He put out the word that people should bring their wagons and come prepared to camp for the duration. Many historians identify this as the first camp meeting, though the term was not used until late in 1802. A large clearing was cut in the woods, and preaching stands and primitive benches were erected. In spite of all the preparations, no one was quite prepared for the actual size of the crowd. Over 10,000 people attended! To grasp how much of a miracle this was, consider that the largest town in Kentucky at the time was Lexington—which numbered 1,800 inhabitants and was over 100 miles away! The crowd at Gasper River was so huge that several of the ministers could preach at the same time. And, as at Red River, "the power of God seemed to shake the whole assembly." McCready exulted, "No person seemed to wish to go home—hunger and sleep seemed to affect nobody—eternal things were the vast concern. Here awakening and converting work was to be found in every part of the multitude; and even some things strangely and wonderfully new to me."

Signs and Wonders

McCready was not alone in his amazement at the strange things taking place by God's Spirit. Even Barton Stone, who had traveled for a week to take part in the revival, was astonished.

"The scene was new to me and passing strange. Many, very many, fell down as men slain in battle and continued for hours in an apparently breathless and motionless state . . . After lying there for hours, they obtained deliverance. They would rise, shouting deliverance, and then would address the surrounding multitude in language truly eloquent and impressive. With astonishment did I hear men, women, and children declaring the wonderful works of God, and the glorious mysteries of the Gospel."

John McGee said, "The mighty power and mercy of God was manifested. The people fell before the word, like corn before a storm of wind, and many rose from the dust with a divine glory" upon their faces. This experience of people "falling" under the Spirit or the Word of God seems to be one of the most remarkable signs attending these revivals. Since so many of the leaders referred to the fallen as being "slain," the phrase "slain in the Spirit" began to circulate, a term still in use today.

The experience of being slain was not the only evidence of an overwhelming work of God. Barton Stone, who called being slain the "falling exercise," also spoke of the jerks, the dancing exercise, the barking exercise, the laughing exercise, the running exercise (performed by onlookers who began to feel their own bodies affected), and the singing exercise. This latter occurred when some began to "sing most melodiously, not from the mouth or nose, but entirely from the breast. It was most heavenly. None could ever be tired of hearing it."

The meeting came to an end, but the revival continued. The attendees returned to their towns and churches and immediately began to organize camp meetings. Throughout Tennessee, Kentucky, Ohio, and even into Virginia, revival fires roared. The most famous of all of these was the celebrated Cain Ridge revival led by Barton Stone. Almost unbelievably, over 20,000 people attended the meeting in 1801, and the signs and wonders were even beyond those Stone had witnessed with McCready.

Unfortunately, as with most great revivals throughout history, men tainted the work of the Spirit. When some sought to surpass the early "exercises" which occurred by the Spirit, excesses set in and the meetings became fleshly and unruly. At the same time, division set in. Doctrinal disputes, which had nothing to do with the work of the Spirit, began to divide the very denominations that had experienced fresh unity. Some with overheated imaginations added to the confusion by preaching new and unbiblical ideas. Barton Stone's sad summary of these troubled times might well be used to describe similar times all through Church history: "These blessed effects would have continued, had not men put forth their hallowed hands to hold up their tottering ark, mistaking it for the ark of God."

The Legacy

It would be difficult to overestimate the impact of the revival in Logan County. It not only gave birth to thousands of smaller revivals like it and some larger like Cain Ridge, but it also contributed "new measures" like the anxious bench, the protracted meeting, and the camp meeting. Charles Finney would use each of these with great impact in the next decades. Frontier religion was shaped for decades by these revivals, particularly as waves of pioneers drank in the revival spirit while passing from the east through Tennessee and Kentucky to the west. The concept of revival as an agent of social change became a part of American religion, as did the themes of individual conversion, denominational unity, miracles, and the priority of preaching.

One surprising result of the revival was its impact on American music, particularly the later rise of country music experiencing such popularity today. Historian Bill Malone in his book, *Country Music USA,* explains:

"Camp meeting songs or songs inspired by them began to appear in books soon after the earliest Kentucky revivals, and both their theology and their structure have endured as part of the fabric of southern religious music and country music. Simple, singable melodies and song texts characterized by choruses, refrains, and repetitive phrases have always been obvious characteristics of country music."

Perhaps the greatest potential lesson from the Logan County revivals is that of the necessity of prayer. A leader in the first Great Awakening, Jonathan Edwards, had taught that when God determines to grant his people revival, He sets them to prayer. Truly, the Second Great Awakening was born on the wings of devoted intercession. Perhaps more than any other theme found in the recorded praises offered to God for granting revival, the fact that He is a "prayer hearing" God is mentioned most often.

In the approach of James McCready, we find an unshakable reliance upon prayer. He was personally devoted to prayer and fasting, and his use of the Covenant of Prayer, whether he knew it or not, has been a means of preparing for revivals the world over. In addition, his emphasis upon repentance as part of intercession, the power of agreement in prayer, and the value of persistence in prayer are lessons which demand attention in our own desperate times.

The fact that the first signs of revival were accompanied by a "spirit of prayer and supplication" only confirms that God grants revival to those "watchman on the walls" who "never hold their peace day and night" and "give Him no rest," seeking "times of refreshing from the presence of God."

Back to the Future: The Meaning of the 1960's

Remember that every generation lives in the wake of their ancestors, in the legacy of those who came before them. This means, as we've seen, that to understand our times we have to understand what past generations have left us—good, bad, or otherwise. The generation of the 1960s was pivotal. Nothing about American society is the same now as it was before that amazing time.

As you read this article, ask yourself how the sixties helped to produce the world you see around you. How has its spiritual legacy touched your life? Focus particularly on the spiritual battles of that decade. In what way are we still fighting those battles today? How can you live more effectively by knowing what happened in the sixties?

The joke is that if you remember the 1960s, you weren't really there. But the truth is that we are all living in the spiritual wake of that perilous decade—whether we remember it or not. If we can take a fresh look, then, at the forces that attached themselves to us during that heartrending time, we will be better able to deal compassionately and effectively with the impact of that era upon our own.

To understand the spiritual climate of the 1960s, we should recall that the years prior to that decade were filled with a suffocating materialism. The Great Depression and World War II had meant sixteen years of hardship for

Americans, who, with war's end, gave explosive vent to a craving for the trophies of technological advance and military victory. For several decades following the war, the American dream would be bound up with the "GI Bill," a frame house in the suburbs, cars with huge fins, the technology of comfort, and, in short, "the good life." We perhaps remember the values of this age best from the film clips of the June Cleaver-type housewife proudly displaying her "modern, space age" kitchen—the promise of a strong and noble society reflected in every shiny appliance.

The children of the World War II generation, those we now call "Baby Boomers," came of age in this era of triumphant materialism and found it without remedy for the aching emptiness in their souls. Sadly, the churches, filled as they were with the spirit of the age, offered no alternatives. The cultural Christianity so loosely woven through their parents' lives was too inconsistently external for this younger generation, desperate as they were for transforming spiritual reality.

This was, after all, the age of Eisenhower—a President who movingly proclaimed a national day of prayer and fasting only to spend it playing golf. Ike had declared his belief that religion is essential to a republic, but then added, "and I don't care what that religion is!" Though it was during the Eisenhower administration that the phrase "In God We Trust" became the national motto, the place for God in the American psyche was tragically small. The post-war generation, entering adulthood as they were in the late fifties and early sixties, were hungering for an invisible reality they could not define and to which their parents seemed completely oblivious. Their discontent was already being heard in the writings of Allen Ginsberg and Jack Kourac, in films like Marlon Brando's *The Wild One,* and in an innocuous philosophy of non-conformity called "Beat."

With the beginning of the 1960s, three events occurred that set the stage for the devastating blows the decade would bring. These were the birth of the Charismatic movement, the rise of Kennedy, and the removal of prayer from the public schools.

The first of these events resulted from the tender response of the heart of God to young America's quiet desperation. In the latter part of 1959, Rev. Dennis Bennett, a neo-orthodox Episcopalian priest in Van Nuys, California, received the Baptism of the Holy Spirit, an experience long believed by most Christians to be a uniquely first century phenomenon. News of this joyfully transforming experience spread rapidly in the 1960s, particularly through the youth culture of the West coast and then through it to the youth of the nation. What came to be known as the "Charismatic movement" had begun, and so had the battle to fill the immense spiritual vacuum of American society.

Then in 1961 forty-four-year-old, Harvard-educated John F. Kennedy became the thirty-fifth president of the United States. Kennedy captured the hearts of the Baby Boomers unlike any other president, largely because the presidents they had known—Roosevelt, Truman, and Eisenhower—had been distant grandfather figures to them. Kennedy seemed to be one of them—a handsome war hero and prize-winning author whose poetic, almost evangelistic, speeches called them to join in changing their world. Kennedy referred to Scripture more than any president in American history, but he changed the quotations to speak of democracy, freedom, and the American way of life. He spoke religiously of America's "calling" to venture into outer space, conquer poverty, win against Communism, and take global responsibility through a program called the "Peace Corps." Youth. Idealism. The New Frontier. Camelot revisited. Kennedy's vision, naive and humanistic though it was, caused young America to believe they could change the world in their own strength, and they never saw the world or themselves in quite the same way again.

The third of these critical events is often overlooked. In the spirit of Kennedy's self-sufficient humanism, the United States Supreme Court, in the 1962 *Engel v. Vitale* case, told 39,000,000 American school children that the twenty-two word prayer with which they started their day was a violation of the Constitution. The offending prayer: "Almighty God, we acknowledge our dependence upon Thee, and we beg Thy blessings upon us, our parents, our teachers, and our Country" seemed innocuous enough. But the result of its removal, as David Barton has so clearly shown in his *America: To Pray or Not to Pray,* was that almost every area of American life mentioned in the prayer began to show unprecedented decline. Statistics on academic test scores, school violence, child abuse, teen pregnancies, alcoholism, violent crime, sexually transmitted diseases, to name just a few, all revealed that the ruling principles of American life had changed dramatically. A wall of protection, constructed through prayer over several generations, was being dismantled.

Thus, with the stage set by an intensified spiritual battle, the illusory hopes of secularism, and a weakened prayer defense, the first of the hammer blows occurred. November 22, 1963. The images are still clear in our minds decades later. Breathless announcers interrupting the broadcast day. Jacqueline's pink dress and pillbox hat. The final announcement from Parkland Hospital. The shock of the nation. Little John-John tearfully saluting his father's casket as the caisson rolled by. The televised assassination of the President's assassin.

The much-debated question of who shot John Kennedy in Dallas' Dealy Plaza is not nearly as important as what it did to the nation. It was a collective trauma on an unprecedented scale, as though the whole nation had experienced a violent accident with all the fear, the uncontrollable emotion, and the desperate search for normalcy that follows such horrors. The gaping national wound that the death of Kennedy left on the American soul meant a loss of the troubled innocence which had characterized post-war society. Now, with the Prince of Camelot slain, the young knights of Camelot were set adrift.

Then began the seduction of a generation. A mere ten weeks after the Kennedy assassination, a deceptively camouflaged assault team landed at LaGuardia Airport in New York. Their alibi for entering the country was to appear on the Ed Sullivan show, riding a crest of popularity from hit songs like "Please

Please Me," "She Loves You," and "I Want to Hold Your Hand." From the very beginning they electrified young America, as films from their concert at Shea Stadium depict. Screaming, weeping, contorting youths were moved by forces beyond the music. Sixteen-year-old girls charged the stage, flattening policemen twice their size, while others simply passed out and had to be carried from the field. No one seemed more stunned by the commotion than the "fab four" themselves, but their music had touched the mourning hearts of Camelot's lonely young knights and now the Beatles would become, however unwittingly, the generals—or perhaps just the sergeants—in a new kind of war.

Having hooked American youth as cute "mopped-topped" boys, the Beatles then underwent a transformation powered by drugs, sex, eastern religions, pop-culture social consciousness, and superstar cynicism. This radical change can clearly be seen in the *Rubber Soul* album of 1965 and the *Sgt. Pepper's Lonely Hearts Club Band* album of 1967. The "four gay lads," as John Lennon once described them, had died. The picture of four graves on the cover of *Sgt. Pepper's* made this point emphatically clear for those who hadn't heard it in the music. What arose in the place of the early Beatles were psychedelic Pied Pipers who played their entire generation into a spiritual abyss.

The "new" Beatles led a bewildered army of millions into mind-altering chemicals, sexual experimentation, and eastern mysticism—this last emphasis a result of their relationship with the Maharishi Mahesh Yogi. By the time John Lennon quipped that the Beatles were more popular than Jesus Christ, he was, sadly, more right than he understood. The disciples of these new Pied Pipers had long ago discarded their parents' seemingly irrelevant Christianity and had begun, at the urging of Beatles' friend, Timothy Leary, to "turn on, tune in, drop out."

The problem with Leary, the Beatles, and the other gurus of that era is that they seldom understood the forces they invoked. As they urged the recreational use of psychedelic drugs, they were unaware that ancient cultures had also used such drugs, but for radically different purposes—to deaden the rational mind and thus open the soul to the influence of spirits. Hallucinogenic drugs for any other purpose was unknown before the 1960s. In fact, the biblical word "witchcraft" is often a translation of the Greek word *pharmakeia*, the term from which we get our words like "pharmacy" and "pharmaceuticals." Without ever fully understanding it, the Beatles and their ilk had pried open a huge door to the demonic, merging culture and the occult in a manner that would reshape their world. It was only the beginning.

And now it seemed that the world was beginning to unravel. In response to a Viet Cong attack on an American compound in South Vietnam, President Lyndon Johnson ordered a massive buildup of American ground troops and the continuous bombing of North Vietnam below the twentieth parallel. It was February of 1965. By the end of the year, there would be a U.S. force of almost 200,000 in Vietnam. At Berkeley, the Free Speech Movement led by Mario Savio escalated dramatically; and before the year was out, sizable student protests in

Manhattan, Oakland, and at the University of Wisconsin signaled the beginnings of a larger movement. On October 15, twenty-two-year-old David J. Miller burned his draft card. And by the Saturday after Thanksgiving, over 20,000 marched on Washington shouting, "Hey! Hey! LBJ! How many kids did you kill today?" The fires were starting to burn, but not just in protest of the war.

The fires were also burning that year in the Watts section of Los Angeles where blacks rioted for six days. They were burning, too, on a stretch of highway between Selma and Montgomery in Alabama, where Martin Luther King led one of the most symbolically important marches in civil rights history. And the fires burned in the hearts of those who mourned the shooting death of Malcolm X as he spoke of racial unity at Manhattan's Audubon Ballroom. In a very different way, the fires also burned within the dominions of the Secret Empire, the Ku Klux Klan, which enjoyed the greatest membership growth in its history this same year.

No two issues would tear at the American soul like Vietnam and race. At the core these problems were questions which challenged all that men had believed about themselves, their leaders, and even the idea of America itself. Americans were beset by a nagging sense that they had been living a lie, that their patriotic ideals and symbols somehow masked a more greedy and viciously oppressive reality. The world had suddenly become a less certain, somewhat lonelier place.

It was during this chaos—for it is chaos which so often gives birth to evil—that he first emerged. He had been an obscure police photographer and a carnival organist. But when he shaved his head, put on a clerical collar, and proclaimed the dawn of the Age of Satan on April 30, 1966, the occult holiday of Walpurgisnacht, Anton Szandor LaVey became the Black Pope of the New Age. His philosophy was rooted in hedonism, the teaching of Aleister Crowley, and the Black Arts, and his gospel of indulgence over abstinence struck a resonant chord in an already self-worshipping culture. His newly formed "Church of Satan" called its adherents to relish "all of the so-called sins, as they all lead to physical, mental, or emotional gratification," and The Satanic *Bible* proclaimed "death to the weakling, wealth to the strong."

LaVey commanded wide media attention with his Black Mass celebrations, "majickal" rituals, and the "baptism" of his daughter in 1967—the recording of which was sold as a record the next year. He served as a consultant on the set of Roman Polanski's ground-breaking occult saga *Rosemary's Baby,* a film about the forced breeding of the devil's child. Polanski's wife, Sharon Tate, would later be murdered by the Charles Manson Gang in the Tate/Labianca "Helter-Skelter" murders. In a not-too-surprising twist, Manson's "family" of assorted misfits was strongly influenced by the teachings of the Black Pope himself, Anton LaVey.

LaVey and his "Magic Circle" of followers legitimized Satanism. When a U.S. Navy seaman who had been a member of the church died, LaVey officiated at the funeral, accompanied by a Navy Honor Guard. The United States government eventually provided its chaplains with a handbook describing the religious needs of Church of Satan members. The IRS granted tax-exempt status to the church, and its local branches began to appear on traditional Church directories.

Before LaVey's popularity began to wane he had become a demonic guru to thousands, including such luminaries as Sammy Davis, Jr., Jane Mansfield, and the rock group The Eagles. By the end of 1967, the Rolling Stones would begin recording an album entitled *Their Satanic Majesties Request,* launching a new era of satanic rock and "horror arts." The Beatles had opened the door and Anton LaVey had walked through it. There would be many others to follow.

From 1967 the pace of change began to be almost overwhelming. Over 475,000 troops were then in Vietnam. The bombing of Hanoi was fully underway. Before long, the Tet Offensive would transform the way American society as a whole viewed the Vietnam War. Thurgood Marshall was sworn in as the country's first black Supreme Court Justice, but ghetto violence peaked. During the long, hot summer months of 1967, over 114 cities in thirty-two states experienced race riots, resulting in eighty-eight dead, 4,000 wounded, and 12,000 arrested. The property damage from one riot alone would total $400,000,000.

But the beat goes on. It was the great year of the hippie. On Easter Sunday, 10,000 youths assembled in New York's Central Park to toss Frisbees, join hands in "love circles," paint their faces, and chant "Banana! Banana!" On this same day in San Francisco, Dr. Timothy Leary called his audience to drop out of society and follow him. Nudity was chic. Twiggy was all the rage. The mini-skirt was a hit. The Beatles released their *Sgt. Pepper's Lonely Hearts Club Band* album, and the film version of *Magical Mystery Tour* was in the theaters. The rock musical *Hair* proclaimed the "Age of Aquarius." Drugs of choice were: DMT, mescaline, methedrine, LSD, and marijuana.

Soon, old wounds were reopened. On April 4, 1968, a shot was fired from a 30.06 Remington pump rifle into a black man standing on the balcony of the Lorraine Motel in Memphis. The man was Dr. Martin Luther King, Jr. The death of Mahatma Ghandi's non-violent disciple was attended by the worst outburst of arson, looting, and criminal activity in the nation's history. Almost two months later to the day, on the first anniversary of the 1967 Israeli-Arab conflict, a vehemently anti-Semitic Jordanian man emptied his snub-nose Iver-Johnson revolver in the direction of a pro-Israel U.S. senator running for president. The senator was Robert Kennedy. Somehow not even the music would soothe the pain this time.

By this point in the decade most Americans were suffering the spiritual equivalent of shell shock. The pummeling blows just kept coming. To cope, some retreated into memories of an earlier time, momentarily forgetting that they had long before abandoned the values which had produced those "better times." Others, believing that the future belonged to the youthful counterculture, simply sailed with the prevailing winds. A larger majority, however, attempted to mask their fear with the brand of cynical humor typified by the hit television series *Laugh In*. But nearly all Americans shared the haunting feeling that an age of innocence had forever passed, and that America could never go home again.

The high water mark of the counterculture was the Woodstock Festival of August, 1969. Over 400,000 people assembled at Max Yasgur's 600-acre dairy farm in the Catskills to hear performances by heroes like Jefferson Airplane, Credence Clearwater Revival, Sly and the Family Stone, Jimi Hendrix, Joan Baez, and Janis Joplin. Despite the rain and woeful lack of food, water, or sanitation facilities, such a strong sense of unity, cooperation, and belonging pervaded the whole affair that Abbie Hoffman aptly dubbed the assembly "the Woodstock Generation." The myth of the "Woodstock Nation" was born.

But the "rush" of Woodstock was short-lived. On December 1, the story of the Tate/Labianca murders hit the papers. The harsh truth wrapped much of the counterculture into an untidy package with the most horrid of murders. As Gary North has written in *Unholy Spirits,* "Charles Manson, who was the friend of rock stars (including, as it later was revealed, several of the Beach Boys, who had actually recorded one of his songs), turned out to be a vicious con artist who used drugs, mysticism, occultism, Beatles' lyrics, Hermann Hesse's pop classic in Eastern mysticism, Siddhartha, sexual debauchery, and other mind-altering techniques to create a dedicated little band of revolutionaries and murderers. The counterculture began to look fearful to millions of people."

It was about to get worse. The day after the grand jury hearings on Manson, a free Rolling Stones concert took place at the

Altamont Speedway near San Francisco. It had been billed as "Woodstock West" and more than 300,000 attended. Fittingly, the Hell's Angels motorcycle gang had been hired to provide security. As Mick Jagger, the Stones' gyrating, taunting lead singer, launched into one of the group's classics, "Sympathy for the Devil," a member of the Hell's Angels stabbed to death a young black man. Jagger stopped singing to calm the commotion in the crowd and remarked, "We always have something very funny happen when we start that number."

The incident was captured by cameras and shown to the world in the motion picture *Gimme Shelter*. As Stones biographer Philip Norman has written, "There, at last, was the crucial moment at Altamont in the red spotlit dark, as Mick Jagger stood, helpless among the real demons his masquerade had summoned up." Like Jagger, the children of the 1960's were beginning to realize the dark side of the forces that they had invoked and that now entangled them.

Then, in 1970, the naive vision and hope of the newly christened Woodstock Nation came, finally, to a jarring end. Within months of Woodstock, Janice Joplin, Jimi Hendrix, and Jim Morrison were dead; the Beatles had disbanded; and the bloodshed of Kent State had virtually ended student protest around the country. An economic recession made jobs for college graduates scarce and soon the realities of the "straight" world began to dawn on the counterculture. Disillusionment built upon disillusionment as the Watergate scandal, the invasion of Cambodia, the Paris Peace talks, and the "urban race wars" filled the headlines. Soon the disco craze and "stagflation" would mark the 1970s. The nearest event to ever again approach a Woodstock-style gathering would be Bob Dylan's concert for 150,000 "people of uncertain sex" on the Isle of Wight in the English Channel! When it was all over, the concert promoters found that they were bankrupt, and so, it appeared to many, was the age itself.

What lessons, then, are we as believers living in this new century to learn from the 1960s? There are many, but perhaps those most relevant to our present crisis are the following.

We must first understand with compassion that what the youth culture of the sixties sought so desperately was what the Church ought to have been. They sought an environment free from the stifling conformity of the outside world. They hungered to live as part of a genuinely open and caring community in which a selfless sharing of lives and possessions could be experienced. Above all, they believed that the invisible is what gives meaning to the visible. What the post-war generation really wanted, though they could hardly have known it, was the gospel of Jesus and the Church it produces. Had the Church been more than a sanctifier of societal values, the kidnapping of a generation might have been prevented.

It is also important that we recognize how spiritual forces of evil attached themselves to our society during the sixties. The youth culture's underlying philosophy of rebellion, eastern mysticism, experimentation with hallucinogenic drugs, wide-ranging sexual excesses, and generational strife all opened the door of our culture to demonic infiltration. Many of the social problems of concern to Christians today have their origins in the pathways to the occult opened by the sixties counterculture. Yet, armed with this knowledge and the weapons of spiritual warfare like the Word of God, repentance, and unified prayer, we can begin to more effectively pull down spiritual strongholds in our land.

Another lesson to be learned from the sixties is that of the vital role of music and the arts in shaping lives. Whatever evil may have been served by some of the music of this era, there has seldom been a more honest, soul-searching, or creative time of musical expression. Not since Martin Luther wrote Christian lyrics for the tunes of German drinking songs had music reflected so much of the heart and passion of a people as did the music of the sixties.

The same can be said of fashion, painting, plays, film, and all of the many "pop arts" which flourished at the time. Had spiritual forces beyond their control—indeed beyond their understanding—not brought the innocence of the early sixties to an end, the artistic expressions of the counterculture might well have remolded the majority of American society. This is true in spite of the fact that few in the counterculture possessed any systematic worldview or any rational apologetic for the kind of culture they were seeking. The medium became the message, and this is so valuable a lesson for Christians living in what is unquestionably an age of symbolism.

Finally, we must recognize that the spiritual battle of the sixties was primarily about the control of that strategic postwar generation. Even today, it is their values and needs which predominantly shape everything in American society from fashion to public policy. Given that the fastest growing segment of American society is among those ninety years of age and older, we can expect the baby boomers to set the pace in our society for decades to come. Clearly, God still wants to redeem that hungry generation. If the Church today can reach that generation and build on their strengths without catering to the self-centered pettiness which has so marked them of late, the impact of the gospel upon American society will be long lasting.

The lyric of a recent country music song complains, "the nineties are the sixties turned upside down." But that may not be a bad thing, if the Church learns "the future of the sixties."

Let the Journey Begin!*

Okay, so maybe now, after all you've read, you can see that history really is more than dates and dead people. If so, it's time for you to explore the far off country of the past for yourself. Now finding a book on history isn't hard *at all* these days. There are *plenty* of great book-stores, online services, and trendy little coffee shops with tragically chic collections of amazingly artsy reads.

But seriously, finding good books written from a distinctly Christian perspective can be a bit of a challenge. So, before I leave you with some parting thoughts, let me help you out. What follows is a list of books, videos, magazines, web sites, and organizations that will help you see history through Christian eyes and, hopefully, live a deeper more meaningful life for what you know. So jump in . . . and don't forget to have some fun along the way.

---

* All books and videos suggested in this chapter are available through www.amazon.com or similar on-line services.

Five Books to Get You Started

1. *The Light and the Glory,* by Peter Marshall and David Manuel (Old Tappan, NJ: Fleming H. Revell Company, 1977) ISBN 0800708865. First published at a time when the United States was still reeling from Vietnam and Watergate, this book identifies the true meaning of America in the faith of the early settlers of this country. It reads like an inspiring novel and covers the almost forgotten time from Columbus to the Constitution. This is both excellent history and a great read. Suggestion: start here.

2. *From Sea to Shining Sea,* by Peter Marshall and David Manuel (Old Tappan, NJ: Fleming H. Revell Co., 1986) ISBN 0800753089. This second in the series by these skilled story-tellers takes you from the uncertain times following the writing of the Constitution to the Civil War. Heroes of the faith like Charles Finney and John Quincy Adams sound forth from these pages, and tales of the Alamo and the Great Awakening are told with fire and grit. History is presented as the unfolding divine drama that it really is.

3. *The Church in History,* by B. K. Kuiper (Grand Rapids, MI: Wm. B. Eerdman's Publishing Company, 1951) ISBN 0802817777. Brace yourself! This is a textbook! But it is also one of the finest introductions to church history you'll find. It's written in a free-flowing style with pictures and charts on most every page, as well as easy-to-absorb short chapters. The

questions at the end of each chapter and section are great for individual review, family discussion, or class assignment. This is definitely the place to begin learning about the history of the Christian faith.

4. *John Wesley,* by John Pollock (Cincinatti, OH: Harold Shaw Publishers, 1995) ISBN 0877884242. The life story of a dynamic man or woman can provide a fascinating window into the past. Biographies and autobiographies make history personal for us. We not only learn but we grow as we "experience" the lives of those who have gone before us. John Pollock has penned some of the best Christian biographies available. Not only has he written this excellent book on John Wesley, one of the men who led England into a transforming season of spiritual renewal, but he has also produced *The Master: A Life of Jesus, Amazing Grace: John Newton's Story, Wilberforce* (about the Christian who almost single-handedly drove slavery from the British Empire), *The Apostle* (about St. Paul), and many other excellent life studies.

5. *The Patriot's Handbook,* by George Grant (Nashville, TN: Cumberland House Publishing, 1996) ISBN 1888952032. George Grant is an award-winning Christian historian whose more than forty books show us how the past explains the present so as to reveal the future. In *The Patriot's Handbook,* Grant has compiled sermons, poems, speeches, and documents from America's past in such a skillful fashion that the soul of the nation is wondrously laid bare. Books such as these are important to our understanding of history because the historical

record is more than just what historians write. It is also what men and women have written as they fulfilled their destinies. When we read works like this, we not only understand the past from the words of those who lived it but we better understand the forces that shape our own times, as well.

What to Read When You're Really Getting Serious!

1. *Church History in Plain Language,* by Bruce Shelley (Dallas: Word Publishing, 1995) ISBN 0849938619. This book is just what its title says it is—an easy to read history for the average guy. Shelley is a professor of Church History, but he knows how to reach the beginner. The short chapters and the reading list at the end of each section are very helpful, and Shelley's gentle, non-technical approach makes this a joy ride through time.

2. *The Day Christ Died,* by Jim Bishop (San Francisco: HarperCollins Publishers, 1957/1977) ISBN 0883658305. This fascinating history of events surrounding the crucifixion of Jesus is made all the more impressive because the author was a noted journalist in his day. He wrote with the clarity and moving simplicity that characterizes not only good journalism but also great literature. This book is sure to draw you into Scripture like few books have. As with other books in this list, this one is recommended not only because it is great reading but also because it shows us a different style of historical writing.

3. *Leaders in Action,* a series edited by George Grant (Nashville, TN: Cumberland House Publishing). As we have seen, the secular approach to the past often ignores the influence of faith in history. This series of books attempts to reveal how Christian faith influenced the lives of famous leaders who are not normally remembered for their spirituality. Each book begins with a short biography of a great leader and then continues with thirty vignettes that explain the pillars of the leader's greatness in light of his Christian faith. A closing section expounds the leader's legacy and impact on modern life. The books in the series are:

    a. *Never Give In: The Extraordinary Character of Winston Churchill,* by Stephen Mansfield (that's me!!), ISBN 1888952199.

    b. *Give Me Liberty: The Uncompromising Statesmanship of Patrick Henry,* by David J. Vaughan, ISBN 1888952229.

    c. *Carry a Big Stick: The Uncommon Heroism of Theodore Roosevelt,* by George Grant, ISBN 1888952202.

    d. *Call of Duty: The Sterling Nobility of Robert E. Lee,* by J. Steven Wilkins, ISBN 1888952237.

    e. *Not a Tame Lion: The Spiritual Legacy of C. S. Lewis,* by Terry W. Glaspey, ISBN 1888952210.

    f. *Then Darkness Fled: The Liberating Wisdom of Booker T. Washington,* by Stephen Mansfield (me again!), ISBN 1581820534.

g. *For Kirk and Covenant: The Stalwart Courage of John Knox,* by Douglas Wilson, ISBN 1581820585.

4. *Grand Illusions: The Legacy of Planned Parenthood,* by George Grant (Nashville, TN: Cumberland House Publishing, 2000) ISBN 1581820577. History gives us a road map to the present. It teaches us how we got here. The wise man will use history to understand the times in which he is called to live. In this award-winning book, George Grant skillfully tells us the story of Planned Parenthood and its founder, Margaret Sanger. In so doing, he gives us a perfect example of how history exposes the vital hidden truths of our times. Not only will you experience a uniquely powerful brand of historical writing but you will also find perspective on some of the most important issues of our times. That is exactly what history viewed in Christian perspective should do.

5. *The 100 Most Important Events in Church History,* by Kenneth Curtis, J. Stephen Lang, Randy Peterson (Grand Rapids, MI: Fleming H. Revell Co., 1999) ISBN 0800756444. Though any ranking of events in history is a debatable project, books like this can help us lift the most critical events from the surging seas of time. This approach can help to sharpen our understanding of the past and also help us to think critically, to analyze, and to strive to understand how the past forms a highway to the present.

The Really Fun Stuff: Learning from Historical Fiction

Good historical fiction is a great way to learn about the past. If the more traditional history book is like flying over the landscape of the past, historical fiction gives us an on-the-ground, three-dimensional view that deepens our understanding and increases our respect for what has come before. Good historical fiction also has the power to fill us with the passion and poetry of days gone by.

One problem may be, though, how do you decide what historical fiction is? In one sense, every novel is "historical" in that it takes place in an historical period. But true historical fiction, the kind I am recommending here, is an attempt to re-tell a true past as accurately as possible using fictional characters, events, and dialogue only to the extent necessary to build a bridge from the past to the present. This kind of fiction gives us "painless" learning wrapped in the excitement of a great novel. Check out these books for starters and then branch out on your own. Enjoy!

1. *Pontius Pilate,* by Paul L. Maier (Grand Rapids, MI: Kregel Publications, 1968) ISBN 0825432960. As the title suggests, this novel is about the man who sentenced Jesus Christ to death, but it is also an exploration of the first century world. Maier is both a gifted writer and a professor of Ancient History, which together make this novel just what you want in good historical fiction: relevance, historical accuracy, skilled storytelling, and depth. Maier followed this novel with *The Flames*

of Rome, the story of the Roman Empire under Nero. Together these books offer a fascinating window into Roman history behind the New Testament.

2. *Druids,* by Morgan Llywelyn (New York: Ivy Books, 1993) ISBN 0804108447. This is the kind of secular novel that Christians ought to be reading. We are living at a time when there is a revival of Celtic spirituality, both secular and Christian. This novel tells the story of Druid spirituality and history in a gritty, moving, and learned fashion. Through Llywelyn's work, we understand not only the past, but also our own times and the nature of the spiritual conflicts Christians will confront in the days to come. In short, by reading this novel, we are not only entertained, but also equipped for battle. We can't ask much more.

3. *Master and Commander,* by Patrick O'Brian (New York: W.W. Norton & Co., 1990) ISBN 0393307050. For adventure, historical accuracy, and beautiful writing, Patrick O'Brian is the master novelist. The series of tales that begins with *Master and Commander* has been touted as the "best historical novels ever written." Like all good books, O'Brian's sea tales can be taken on a variety of levels. They are "ripping good yarns." They are excellent presentations of the Napoleonic worldview. They are accurate representations of naval life in the early 1800s. And, they are masterfully written literature. This is the kind of historical fiction that can help anyone fall in love with the past . . . and the sea!

4. *Joan of Arc,* by Mark Twain (San Francisco: Ignatius Press, 1989) ISBN 0898702682. When you think of Mark Twain, you probably think of *The Adventures of Tom Sawyer* or *Huckleberry Finn.* You may not know that Mark Twain labored for decades on an historical novel about Joan of Arc and thought it would be the book people would most remember him for. Though he was clearly wrong about his legacy, Twain nevertheless produced a beautiful portrait of the French girl who arose by revelation to lead the armies of her land. This is a moving and skillfully told story, bringing to life a woman and an age often ignored in the standard teaching of history. You will probably never think of Mark Twain in the same way again!

5. *Quo Vadis,* by Henryk Sienkiewicz (New York: Hippocrene Books, 1999) ISBN 0781807638. Written in the 1890's, this book was a publishing phenomenon when it first appeared. In fact, for this and several other brilliant novels, Sienkiewicz later won the Nobel Prize for literature. Though on the surface, this novel is the tale of a Roman general's love for a Christian slave girl, the story unfolds in such a way that the history and drama of the first century world is vibrantly revealed. Whether detailing the sadistic persecution of Christians, the vile character of Nero, or the unshakable faith of pagan converts to "The Way," Sienkiewicz has told a story that entertains, teaches, and even infuses *Bible* reading with fresh energy. Read the novel and then rent the video, which is one of the finest representations of first century Rome on film.

Hollywood Does History:
Ten Great Films for Exploring History

Some have said that movies are the literature of our time. Whether this is true or not, the fact is that movies possess amazing power to teach just as they possess amazing power to shape a culture. When it comes to the study of history, movies can be incredibly important because they give us a picture of earlier times we would never "see" otherwise. Since we as humans think in pictures, movies can give us the images and thought-forms that help us think more clearly about the past. Naturally, no film is going to present the past with perfect accuracy, but a good historical film can help us experience history in a truly transforming fashion.

Here are ten films that present the past in an enjoyable, educational, and inspiring manner. Start with these and then visit the "Historical" section of your local video store. Parents, please note the rating on each of these films and determine for yourself if they are suitable for your family to see. A great historical film normally includes all the elements of the age it depicts—moral and immoral. Please be careful.

1. *Chariots of Fire*. This Academy Award-winning film is the moving story of Olympic champion and Christian missionary, Eric Liddell. The film wonderfully captures both post-World War I Europe and the tensions between Christianity and Judaism in an increasingly secular England. The soundtrack alone makes viewing this film worthwhile.

2. *Breaker Morant.* Few people today know much about the Boer War, but the importance of this conflict in the history of warfare, not to mention the history of South Africa, can hardly be exaggerated. Outstanding performances, masterful directing, and some of the finest photography on film makes this a glorious learning experience.

3. *Gallipoli.* For those who lived through the First World War, the Dardanelles disaster had the same impact that the My Lai massacre held for the Vietnam War generation. In retelling an often forgotten story, this film powerfully depicts the loss of innocence at the turn of the century and the horrors of battle in the "War to End all Wars." Since a young Mel Gibson is one of the stars, the movie is a guaranteed thrill.

4. *Glory.* This award-winning film tells the true story of the famous Massachusetts Fifty-Fourth Regiment during the American Civil War. The script is based on the letters and jour-nals of that black Regiment's white colonel, Robert Gould Shaw. The film movingly presents the worldview of that era and the carnage of the War Between the States in a particularly skillful fashion. Denzel Washington won an Academy Award for his powerful performance in this masterpiece.

5. *Cromwell.* Though the fact that this movie was made in 1970 definitely shapes its perspective (Cromwell is heard to tout the cause of democracy, something he would have abhorred), it is nevertheless a fascinating look at the issues of

the time and the character of the "Lord Protector of the Realm." Since the English Civil War is so little understood in our day, this film provides a valuable service in making the critical issues of the conflict understandable to a modern audience. The depiction of England in the 1600s is incredibly accurate and helpful.

6. *The Lighthorsemen.* This film is both an exciting war story and an introduction for most viewers to a little known or understood theatre of World War I. Excellent performances, bold photography, and the tender treatment of individual characters all make this a favorite.

7. *Young Winston.* This is not only a superb study of Churchill's life—based directly on his autobiography, *My Early Life*—but is also one of the finest depictions of turn of the century England available. To truly enjoy this film, watch it, then read Churchill's *My Early Life*, and then watch the film again. You'll become inspired to read more on Churchill's life and writings. If so, don't forget *Never Give In,* my favorite book about Churchill . . . even if I did write it!!

8. *Sergeant York.* Sergeant Alvin York was one of the great American heroes to emerge from the First World War. This film not only tells the story of York's war exploits, but also captures his religious conversion and his subsequent wrestling with pacifism. This is a great family film and a wonderful introduction to one of America's heroic figures.

9. *Amistad.* When a Spanish ship was commandeered by it's captive slaves and sailed inadvertently to the coast of the United States, one of the greatest episodes in American legal history began. During a trial to determine ownership of the slaves, which was conducted decades before the Civil War, many of the great issues of slavery and American democracy were explored. This is a powerful film, directed by Steven Spielberg and starring a huge cast of great actors.

10. *Braveheart.* It is hard to exaggerate the long shadow that William Wallace has cast upon western history, particularly the early history of the United States. Even Abraham Lincoln's son was named William Wallace Lincoln! This hugely popular film, though depicting many bloody and violent scenes, gives a sense of the man's greatness and the titanic issues of his times.

Five Fantastic Web Sites for Learning Christian History

The Internet has transformed the study of history just as it has so many other arenas of modern life. If you have a computer with a modem, you have historical resources at your fingertips that rival the great libraries of old. Check out the five web sites listed here and follow up on their recommended links. You might also search for specific topics that interest you by using Internet search engines like altavista.com or hotbot.com.

1.   Christian Classics Ethereal Library
     http://ccel.wheaton.edu/

You can save huge amounts time and money by downloading the hundreds of Christian classics available on this site. The many biographies, autobiographies, and histories make this a wonderful source for Christian history.

2.   The Hall of Church History:
     Theology from a Bunch of Dead Guys
     http://www.gty.org/~phil/hall.htm

Combining great graphics, sound scholarship, and a wacky sense of humor, this site is a wonderful place to delve into the people, ideas, and controversies of Christian history. You won't agree with everything that's said here, but remember, the study of Church History is partially about deciding what you believe and what you don't. This site will help you think through the issues.

3.   Religion and the Founding of the American
     Republic
     http://lcweb.loc.gov/exhibits/religion/

Though the Library of Congress sponsors this site, it is included here because it is a rare admission by a branch of our government that religion is essential to an understanding of the American past. This is an excellent combination of art and text to explain the role of faith in the American colonial period and the American Revolution.

4. Heroes of History
    www.heroesofhistory.com

Heroes are the people who have shaped their generations by breaking through the barriers that kept others bound. This site examines heroes as diverse as George Washington Carver, Mother Theresa, and Billy Graham. This is a good site for learning how to discern the pillars of greatness in the lives of history's heroes.

5. The Spurgeon Archive
    www.spurgeon.org/mainpage.htm

This award-winning site is an excellent example of how a web site can be used to let the past speak to the present. Charles Haddon Spurgeon, often called "The Prince of Preachers," lived in England in the 1800s. He is a powerful example of a noble Christian who challenged the unfaithfulness of his times. Hopefully, this web site will inspire many others like it.

Hitting the Highways: Learning History from Travel

Nothing inflames the imagination quite like walking where history happened. To sit in a seat at Ford's Theatre where Lincoln was shot, to walk the battlefields of the Civil War, to crouch in Churchill's underground "War Room," or to stand on the watchtower of a Crusader castle is to "feel" the past in a unique and life-changing way. Often such history sites include hidden signs of a forgotten Christian heritage that you will want to uncover as you begin exploring history from a biblical perspective. These guides will help you.

1. *God's Signature over the Nation's Capital: Evidence of Your Christian Heritage,* by Catherine Millard (New Wilmington, PA: Son Rise Publications, 1985) ISBN 0936369175. The founder of a Christian tour company in Washington D.C., Catherine Millard is eminently qualified to expose the many signposts of faith in the nation's capital. Did you know that on top of the Washington Monument is an aluminum cap that proclaims, "Praise Be to God?" Did you know that there is a prayer for presidential wisdom inscribed on a mantel in the White House? These and other such symbols of Christian heritage are detailed in this invaluable book. Don't visit Washington D.C. without it!

2. *In God We Trust Tour Guide,* by Stephen McDowell and Mark Beliles (Charlottesville, VA: Providence Foundation, 1998) ISBN 1887456074. This guide not only explains the Christian heritage evident in Washington D.C., but also arms you for travel in Philadelphia and the many historic sites of Virginia. A wonderful companion to Catherine Millard's guide listed above, this book will transform your travels through America's heritage-rich eastern seaboard.

Three Films, a Magazine, and a Preacher
Three Films . . .

1. *How Should We Then Live,* by Francis Schaeffer (Gospel Communication International, Inc., 1-800-GospelDirect; www.1800gospeldirect.com). This groundbreaking film series is a fascinating overview of history from the time of Christ to the present. Philosopher/theologian Francis Schaeffer explains the main philosophical and historical issues of each period and demonstrates how the gospel of Jesus Christ provided the answers for each age.

Filmed on location around the world, *How Should We Then Live* employs some of the most creative photographic techniques ever used in a film of this kind. Every student of history should see this excellent series. A local Christian bookstore or Church resource center will probably have these tapes or you can call Gospel Communication International directly.

2. *Gateway Films Christian Heritage Series* (Gateway Films/Vision Video, P.O. Box 540, Worchester, PA 19490; 1-800-523-0226; www.gatewayfilms.com). Gateway Films/Vision Video distributes this excellent series of videos about the great figures in Church History. These dramatic presentations deal with men like John Wycliffe, John Hus, the Moravians, William Wilberforce, C. S. Lewis, William Tyndale, and others. These are unquestionably the best films about these individuals, and if you cannot find them at your local Christian video store, you can rent them for your Church or study group by calling the number above.

3. *America's Godly Heritage, Education, and the Founding Fathers: Keys to Good Government* by David Barton (Gospel Communication International, Inc., 1-800-GospelDirect; www.1800gospeldirect.com). David Barton is a gifted teacher who has brought America's Christian heritage to national attention through his books and videos. His book *America: To Pray or Not to Pray* tells the story of moral decline after prayer was outlawed in America's public schools. The three videos listed above tell the story of faith and the founding fathers that has been ignored in most retellings of the American past.

A Magazine . . .

Christian History (Christianity Today, Inc., 465 Gundersen Drive, Carol Stream, IL 60188; 1-877-247-4787; www.christianity.net/christianhistory). There are many magazines that include articles on Christian history from time to time, but the only popularly-written Christian magazine that devotes every issue to a single historical topic is Christian History magazine. Past issues have included topics such as religious liberty, William Tyndale, pietism, money, C. S. Lewis, John Wesley, Jonathan Edwards, John Calvin, the Great Awakening, St. Augustine, John Bunyan, and the Baptists. An annual subscription for this quarterly publication is very affordable and all past issues can be purchased on a beautifully designed CD-ROM. It's well worth the investment.

And a Preacher

Dr. D. James Kennedy (Coral Ridge Ministries, 5555 N. Federal Highway, Fort Lauderdale, FL 33308; 1-954-771-8840; www.crpc.org). It may seem strange to include the sermon tapes of a television preacher in a list of resources about Christian history. But Dr. Kennedy is not only a pastor but also a gifted historian. He often preaches on historical topics, and when he does the uniquely Christian perspective with which he approaches the past yields some incredible opportunities to learn. Did you know that Lincoln was talking about Jesus when he was shot? Did you know that Columbus believed it was the Holy Spirit who led him to the New World? Dr. Kennedy's sermons are available in inexpensive booklet form or on audiotape. Some of Dr. Kennedy's sermon titles include "The Faith of Washington," "Was Lincoln a Christian," "The Pilgrims Speak Today," and "America's Godly Heritage."

Five Helpful Organizations

There are a number of organizations that specialize in popularizing the forgotten truths of Christian history. The publications and recommendations of these organizations can be incredibly helpful in your journey toward understanding the past. You can learn more from each organization's web site or by writing to ask for a trial subscription to newsletters and reading list. This is a great way to join the Christian "historical community" nationwide.

1. American Vision (P.O. Box 220, Powder Springs, GA 30127; 1-770-222-7266; www.americanvision.org). American Vision, led by author and lecturer Gary DeMar, publishes a very useful newsletter called "The Biblical Worldview" and has turned out some excellent publications. One of the most unique of their productions is a professionally recorded dramatic overview of the story of Christianity in America.

2. Plymouth Rock Foundation (The Fisk Mill, P.O. Box 577, Marlborough, NH 03455; 1-800-210-4020; www.plymrock.org/PlymrockNewsletters.html). In addition to advocating biblical principles of self and civil government, Plymouth Rock is devoted to acquainting Americans with the blessings of their Christian heritage. This is done through numerous publications and taped productions. Their FAC-Sheet on various contemporary issues is invaluable.

3. Foundation for American Christian Education (F.A.C.E., P.O. Box 9588, Chesapeake, VA 23321-9588; 1-800-352-3223; www.face.net/). This organization has published some of the most important and beautifully bound works on America's Christian heritage. Their video and audiotapes are among the best and they publish a journal that is inspiringly educational.

4. American Christian History Institute (P.O. Box 648, Palo Cedro, CA 96073; 1-530-547-3535; www.achipa.com/index.html). Led by James B. Rose, the Institute sponsors superb

regional training seminars in American Christian history. Topics include principles of American Christian government, education, and American history.

5. Providence Foundation (P.O. Box 6759, Charlottesville, VA 22906; 1-804-978-4535; ww.providencefoundation.com). The application of biblical principles to public life is the goal of this productive foundation. They have developed some very unique tools, like a Christian history guide to Washington D.C. and a board game which teaches American Christian history. They also provide books, videos, cassette tapes, and seminars— all with the purpose of preparing Christians to disciple the nations.

Some Final Words

Okay, we've had some fun. We've learned some things. Maybe we've even been inspired. But let's think about the bigger picture for just a moment.

We are living at a time when the gospel is going out into all the earth like never before. Look at what time it is. Go ahead. Look at your watch or a clock nearby. By this same time tomorrow more people will have become Christians for the first time than during any other twenty-four hour period since Jesus was raised from the dead. It's true!

If that blows your mind, think about this. More than thirty-five percent of everyone who has ever been born again since Jesus was raised from the dead have been born again in the last five years. Isn't that astonishing? There's no question, Christianity is growing more rapidly than ever.

But think for a moment about the people who are coming into the kingdom of God. What have they been told about history? They've been taught the old evolutionary myths. Or perhaps they've had some other strange view of the past planted in their brains.

The truth is, they've been robbed. They've been denied the glorious privilege of understanding the past in light of the God who created it. That means, they've been denied the opportunity to live the exceptional lives that knowing history helps us live. And in a sense, we've all been robbed. Remember what Winston Churchill said: "The greatest advances in human civilization have come when we recovered what we had lost: when we learned the lessons of history." The fact is that as a society, as well as individuals, we must recover the lost lessons of history—the lessons that can only be recovered when we see the past through the eyes of faith.

So now that you've read this little book, you have the tools to help those who are coming into the kingdom find a new understanding of the past. They need to be taught how to see history through a Christian lens. They need help to get connected to the great heritage of faith they have. And they need to let, as C. S. Lewis said, the "fresh sea-breeze of the ages" blow through their lives, refreshing them and lifting them to their best. This is part of making disciples, of helping fellow believers take hold of their destiny.

So whether you are a student in school, an adult long out of school, or a Christian leader, make a knowledge of history in Christian perspective part of your arsenal of faith. Let your Christian heritage ennoble your life and make you more effective in changing your world. Then you can help those who are just stepping into the kingdom take hold of their destiny in part by taking hold of the past that reveals that destiny.

Please, before you close this book, take a moment to read the quotations that follow. Let them stoke your passion to know the past, understand the past, and shape the future armed with the insights of the past.

A people without a heritage are easily persuaded.
—Karl Marx

History must be our deliverer not only from the undue influence of other times, but from the undue influence of our own, from the tyranny of the environment and the pressures of the air we breathe.
—Lord Acton

The greatest advances in human civilization have come when we recovered what we had lost: when we learned the lessons of history.
—Winston Churchill

The only thing new in the world is the history you don't know.
—Harry Truman

A nation which does not remember what it was yesterday, does not know what it is today, nor what it is trying to do. We are trying to do a futile thing if we do not know where we came from or what we have been about. Ours is a rich legacy. Rich but lost.

—Woodrow Wilson

To comprehend the history of a thing is to unlock the mysteries of its present, and more, to disclose the profundities of its future.

—Hilaire Belloc

I make known the end from the beginning, from ancient times, what is still to come. I say: My purpose will stand, and I will do all that I please.

—Isaiah 46:10

History maketh a man old, without either wrinkles or gray hairs; privileging him with the experience of age, without either the infirmities or inconveniences thereof.

—Thomas Fuller

Can righteousness be done in a land of forgetfulness?

—Psalm 88:12

History has a wonderful way of freeing us from the cult of the contemporary.

—Richard J. Foster

What has been will be again, what has been done will be done again; There is nothing new under the sun. Is there anything of which one can say, "Look! This is something new?" It was here already, long ago; it was here before our time.

—Ecclesiastes 1:9–10

Some people live in the present, oblivious of the past and blind to the future. Some dwell in the past. A very few have the knack of applying the past to the present in ways that show them the future. Great leaders have this knack.

—Richard Nixon

The future is always built out of the materials of the past.
—Booker T. Washington

History is philosophy learned from examples.

—Thucydides

The whole of history is incomprehensible without Jesus.
—Ernest Renan

Those who cannot remember the past are condemned to repeat it.
—George Santayana

My heart mused: "Has God forgotten to be merciful? Has he in anger withheld His compassion?" Then I thought, "To this I will appeal: the years of the right hand of the Most High." I will remember the deeds of the Lord; yes, I will remember your miracles of long ago. I will meditate on all your works and consider all your mighty deeds.

—Psalm 77:9–12

History should be a work of art and imagination rather than a dry compendium of facts.

—Theodore Roosevelt

We cannot say the past is past without surrendering the future.
—Winston Churchill

We are inexplicable to ourselves without reference to our history: and this is true both of our individual and of our social life. If I want to know what makes me tick morally, I shall find more illumination from a study of the Puritans than from the most diligent discipline of introspection. And the character of American society is similarly inexplicable without proper attention to the rock from which it was hewn.

—Alexander Miller

Printed in the USA
CPSIA information can be obtained
at www.ICGtesting.com
JSHW082213140824
68134JS00014B/600